PRO TEAMS KUMITESPORT: MARTIAL ARTS
This book is your Exclusive Proposal Edition

You are now free to choose between owning a *Multimillion-Dollar National Sports Team* or one day feeling sorry for yourself for passing up on this opportunity. The difference is a phone call to me so we can all get to know each other—You, myself and 31 other individuals and investor groups who will become the select members of an exclusive group of sports team owners.

As you read this letter, you are also holding this book, **The Exclusive Proposal Edition,** that I am making this opportunity available to like-minded individuals. I have made both this edition, The Exclusive Proposal Edition, and **The Team Players Edition,** available on Amazon.com for the public to enjoy and compare.

Just imagine how successful you would be today if you bought into the NFL during its infancy, unless you're one of the owners in the NFL that I sent this book to. Here is your brand new chance to find yourself into the same opportunity now. As you are holding this book in your hands, visualize owning one of only 32 Pro Sports Team Franchises in the country!

The sport of the 21st century We will have both male and female athletes

You have just discovered what is currently the best opportunity in a fast-growing industry that is exciting, unique and with unlimited upside potential!

This book is everyone's blueprint—feel free and decide to join now because for someone of your knowledge, experience and expertise. this is simply second nature and can be an easy decision. Call me now if you want me to personally introduce you to all of this. Allow yourself to finish reading the book later.

Men and Women in the 21st Century

You may not know this, for over eighty years martial artists have honed their skills in one- on-one martial combat in hopes of being the best of best. So far, no one, including investors, has yet to reap the huge rewards that the sport can generate, should it break out of its current limitations.

At any given time, there are 500 or more martial arts tournament circuits within the United States. At any given time, there could be 500 individual champions for the same weight class and they may never compete against one another to unify a championship. It seems like there is a new circuit established every week.

Just imagine how successful you would be today if you bought into the NFL during its infancy

Besides excelling in a martial arts tournament, being picked up and starring in a movie, or participating in the MMA, there is nothing else for the point martial artist to do to become a superstar. Until now!

Plus keep in mind that we have the sport of the 21st century and we will have both male and female athletes!

Let Us Take Point Martial Arts to a Top-Notch Level

The Pro Teams KumiteSport Martial Arts (PTKMA), our organization, is poised to propel this exciting sport to long-term greatness and international recognition.

We owners and organizers will have standardized regulations and commitments to establish the first ever professional team point martial arts circuit. Under belts will have a point system, and the winners of the 18+ black belt point fighting divisions will represent their state or city team and compete against the other 31 teams within the Pro Teams KumiteSport Martial Arts (PTKMA).

We will all have events culminating into city/state championships across the nation.

Ease into Ownership!

For the past two decades I have been working on positioning point martial arts like other major league sports (NFL, NBA, NHL and or MLB), with franchise teams, with potential team owners like yourself who will enjoy personal or corporate ownership along with the benefits that come with owning a team. You will become one out of 32 teams that can be willed to your heirs.

I have already taken the time and have hired lawyers to franchise the concept so that it is recognized by the U.S. Securities and Exchange Commission (SEC). I have even gone the extra mile to get listed on the Franchise Registry so that any potential owner needing funding can walk into any bank in America and get 80% of their loan backed by the Small Business Administration.

What will you lose if you don't call me at all?

As you own your pro sports team, you are going to be enjoying the profitable benefits of team ownership, i.e. product merchandising, ticket sales, product sponsorship, etc.

You can entertain and offer martial arts school franchises within your territory. You will reap the monetary benefit of receiving circuit fees of all tournaments executed under the Pro Teams KumiteSport Martial Arts National Circuit within your territory.

Remember that your team will be the only one in your state, unless your hunch tells you to be in California, Texas or Florida— big states which can have up to three.

What will you lose if you don't call me now?

You as a team owner will be able to help martial artists realize their dreams of becoming professional black belt athletes. Your goal now will be to find the best competitors within your exclusive territory to compete and secure team positions and bring back the National Championship for your city and state.

There is a deadline for bids, so please be prompt and connect with me soon! Over the next few days, you might be entertaining this in your mind more and more. Base your decisions on your own hunch, experience and expertise in sports.

Don't you remember colleagues who have talked about this pipe dream of owning a sports team? Did you ever get into this huge conversation over a beer on a nice afternoon after a great, memorable game? Just like the NFL, there will be a total of 32 teams here and you can become an owner.

Consider yourself extremely lucky if you own a team exactly like the rest of us here. You know that team ownership isn't for many others. And, before I end this letter, entertain this as well: if you own a team now, you can always auction it off to your own contacts and investors anytime in the future!

You, myself and 31 other individuals and investor groups

Imagine, right now, of being a part of something new and exciting. You have nothing to lose right now if you call me. What will you lose if you don't call me at all?

Sincerely,

Books by
Dexter V. Kennedy

TEAM POINT FIGHTING
In a Professional
Martial Arts League

TEAM POINT FIGHTING
INVESTORS GAME PLAN
In a Professional
Martial Arts League

TAKING ON THE NFL:
The National Martial Arts League

These books have similar content except that the Investors Game Plan has the additional pages introducing this entire idea and system of operations to investors. Everyone has access to all the books, available on Amazon.com. Everyone is encouraged to purchase the first two books.

PRO TEAMS KUMITESPORT
MARTIAL ARTS

DEXTER V. KENNEDY

ISBN 978-1-957781-48-8 (softcover)
ISBN 978-1-958128-71-8 (hardcover)
ISBN 978-1-957781-49-5 (ebook)
Library of Congress Control Number: 2022905014

Ordering Information:
Special discounts are available for quantity purchases by corporations, associations, educators, and others. For details, contact the publisher at the above-listed address.

U.S. trade bookstores and wholesalers:
Please contact Dexter V. Kennedy
Telephone: (803) 665-8453 or
Email: dexterkennedy@hotmail.com

Please go to "Connect with Dexter Kennedy" on page 171 for more contact information.

Graphic design, cover & interior; partial editing by Valentino Zubiri (valzubiri@gmail.com)

We would like to thank the creators of the following fonts which were used in the book:
- Anton, ©2011, Vernon Adams (vern@newtypography.co.uk). This Font Soft ware is licensed under the SIL Open Font License, Version 1.1
- Boardley & CS Nancy, Craft Supply Co. license
- Cagliostro, by MADType, public domain GPL, OFL
- DS Hansen, ©2012 by Typographer Mediengestaltung licensed under the Open Fonts License
- Francois One by Vernon Adams (vern@newtypography.co.uk) licensed under the SIL Open Font License, Version 1.1
- FreeSans & FreeSerif (OTF), General Public License - GNU GPL
- Gabo Drive ©2010 by Dannci licensed under the Open Fonts License
- Gotham & Gotham Black, General Public License - GNU GPL
- Linux Libertine G licensed under the Open Fonts License

Printed in the United States of America.

Book Vine Press
2516 Highland Dr.
Palatine, IL 60067

Dedication

I dedicate this book to my parents, Marshall and Hermetta Kennedy, for whom without I would not be here. To my brother, Marlvis, to my sister Denise and daughters, Rashonda and Sharlene for supporting me, and to my youngest daughter, Eboné, for her support, encouragement and for creating the thirty-two team logos needed for the Pro Teams KumiteSport Martial Arts. Also, my sensei, Mike Genova, the man who taught me in my youth and supported my vision, and to all martial artists who support point martial arts and are seeking a professional level of competition. Most importantly, I would like to thank God for giving me this vision. I finally did it.

WARNING: Everything in this book may be out-of-the-box thinking, but if it is, it's all right!

Preface

This is the newest first printing based on the earlier book, Taking on the NFL: The National Martial Arts League by Mr Dexter V Kennedy (2015).

We encourage everyone to read this book because it has undergone an improved book design and further editing. This book has much better readability and more organized chapters. Taking on the NFL: The National Martial Arts League simply shows earlier date of publication.

The author has decided to keep the first book in circulation because the earlier publication date of the first edition shows an earlier date of release of the original, proprietary and innovative ideas and proposals of Mr. Dexter V. Kennedy.

If you are interested in participating or if you have any further questions, please contact Mr. Dexter V. Kennedy. Contact information is located in "Connect with Dexter Kennedy" on page 171 of this book.

Acknowledgement

A am very grateful, to the accomplished author Valentino Zubiri, whom himself has written over ten books for guiding this work despite his busy schedule with interest. He has made several important suggestions which have tremendously enhanced this edition.

I am deeply indebted to EKGraphix for creating the team logos and more specifically Ebone' Sakoya Kennedy, President, for continuing to update and maintain the quality of these logos as she progressed through her undergrad education.

I am also thankful to my dear friend Mike Genova, my teacher of American karate and one of South Carolina's martial arts hall of famers for the many discussions we had about point martial arts becoming the next big sport.

Most importantly, my mother, for motivating me to return to the martial arts when I needed an activity to get back in shape after my life in Desert Storm.

This work has truly been transformed.

Thank you,

DK

Table of Contents

Introduction

Could point martial arts actually challenge the NFL?

In 1997, I realized the need to get fit. My youngest daughter from my second marriage was five years old, and I had several family deaths due to heart disease and cancer. After the birth of my daughter, I realized more and more, each day, how I wanted to be there for her and see her grow into the beautiful woman she's grown to today. For this reason, my journey began. Eighteen years as of this writing. God birthed into my spirit the concept of a league, in which martial artists would represent their city/ state via team competition in a national championship, which would be called Kumite Sport. I think everyone involved in martial arts knows what Kumite is, as well as, what it's all about.

My primary purposes for writing this book are to:

- Protect my concept

- Introduce it to the martial arts community, and then

- Introduce it to the world

I've spent the last nineteen years of my life researching the possibilities of my total martial arts concept. I've attended and competed in, numerous martial arts tournaments. I've written approved business plans and interviewed an infinite number of martial artists. Although there have been other successful martial arts venues, I still don't think to this day we've touched the tip of the iceberg of the possibilities. One time in America, Golf was the number one sport. I think it's now unquestionable American football is the number one sport in America. If I were to make a prediction for the future, I would say mixed martial arts are the game of the future for America if packaged right.

After eighteen years of researching and developing business plans and franchising, I am now ready to make my concept available to the world through franchising. Since National Football League teams are available through franchising, major league baseball teams are franchised, and national basketball teams are franchises, then why can't world martial arts pro-teams also be franchised? As you read through this book, you'll learn about the steps taken, along with the risks. Also, you will learn about how I've made my concept available through franchising, which I think is the next best natural step toward increasing growth and exposure to martial arts as a sport. Anyone interested in taking this adventure with me in growing point martial arts into a world competition is encouraged to contact me. My contact information can be found in **"Connect with Dexter Kennedy" on page 171.** I welcome all of those willing to take this journey with me.

I, for this reason, write this document hoping to protect and preserve the design, concept and methodology of my American Idol-like professional martial arts venue. At which point martial arts tournament superstars can graduate. It is amazing to me how martial arts has been taught and practiced in America for well over 70 years. Yet there still isn't a national or world sports program similar to that of say soccer with a flavor like MLB, NFL and NBA for martial arts.

Another reason for this book is to make the world aware of my vision in hopes of creating the passion needed to make this dream a reality. Through this book, I will educate martial artists, trainers, health and wellness experts, fitness instructors, investors, and business people on how they too can participate and become successful in this business. Lastly, I hope to obtain the necessary resources to make this opportunity a reality. I would like to take this time to introduce:

PRO TEAMS KUMITE SPORT
Martial Arts League

I retired from United States Army after serving for almost 17 years (March 1, 1994). I decided it was time for me to call it quits after I was "ordered" for yet another combat deployment; this time for Somalia. This book is about what God has put in my spirit, my dream, and my passion in which I'd like to share and protect. All of my life I have had dreams and goals. I think in the military, we are trained to be overachievers. We learn through natural progression. After a certain period of time, the military expects you to make PFC, and there is an expected time to advance to specialist 4, and E5, E6 and so forth. So when a veteran's time in service ends and he or she becomes a civilian, they then look to transition to something similar. Veterans are used to a natural built in career progression system with a clear path for career advancement.

In my quest, I've played football, baseball, basketball. I've boxed for the United States Army, participated in the hundreds of karate tournaments, attended modeling school and played in numerous bands, all in hopes of finding my real gift. Where I have dominion, that talent or skill that would make me great, famous, successful or whatever, you want to call greatness.

I was looking for my domain. As the word says, let them have dominion. I was looking for something I would be in control of and successful at, or the best at, or at least at the top level. Pro Teams KumiteSport is a reboot of Taking on the NFL: The National Martial Arts League which is the book that started it all. A book about my successes and failures in implementing a point martial arts league. It also tells how the Lord blessed me with the concept and vision of the Pro Teams KumiteSport Martial Arts, and what I call the total martial arts concept. Every great person has a story; this is mine.

PTKMA Team Names

THE GOLDEN

EAGLES

THE FIVE

ELDERS

TEN TIGERS

THE KNIGHTS
OF DARKNESS

THE DEATH
SQUAD

THE STREET FIGHTERS

THE GOLDEN

CENTIPEDE

36 FAMILIES

THE WOUKOU

PIRATES

THE

9

DRAGONS

7 CLANS OF HUNG FU

THE MANTID

THE BLACK EMPEROR
SCORPION

THE

SHAOLIN WARRIORS

THE WHITE CRANE

Red Lotus

SNAKE FIST FIGHTERS

THE EIGHT IMMORTALS

THE MIDNIGHT ASSASSINS

THE KOMODO LIZARDS

The Fist Animals

THE DRAGON SOCIETY

OWN THE RIGHTS TO YOUR CITY'S PRO SPORTS TEAM

ONLY 32 TEAMS AVAILABLE

PRO TEAMS KUMITESPORT
MARTIAL ARTS

DEXTER V. KENNEDY

1 The True Origin of Martial Arts

Nijel Binns is the author of the 1990 book *Nuba Wrestling™: The Original Art*. In the book, Binns presents his theory that martial arts originated in the ancient northeast African kingdom of Nubia.

Here I share a few excerpts from his book, *Nuba Wrestling™: The Original Art*.

Millions of African Americans, black and people of color from all over the world study kung fu, taekwondo, judo, karate, or some other form of martial arts. Many of them will tell you that it has transformed their lives. For this reason, books, videos, magazines, television, and films will continue to depict the martial arts. There are even comic book characters such as Karnak, 1960's Marvel superhero, and a member of the mutant group known as the Inhumans. Karnak is a martial arts master who is able to discern the stress point of any solid object, no matter how large, and shatter that object with one powerful and well-placed karate chop.

As popular as the martial arts was and continues to be, less than one percent of Africans in the diaspora and only a slightly higher percentage of Asians and Europeans are aware that the real origins of these magnificent arts are, in fact, African! Many African teens fantasized about becoming the powerful Karnak will be surprised to learn that he was actually named after an ancient African temple in Egypt and that the very name of his old discipline bespoke its origin. It is only recently that modern science and anthropology have agreed to admit that all human life shares a common point of origin in Africa. It was a watershed day. For this reason, when the untold origins of the oldest martial arts on Earth were explored and documented in the book entitled *Nuba Wrestling™: The Original Art*. While not in general circulation, it is heralded as a landmark publication because it was the first global acknowledgment of Africa as the birthplace of the martial arts and sciences.

In the year 2000 of the Olympic Games, there are many people who would argue that Greece contains the oldest records of combative arts such as wrestling, boxing, and Pankration. While the western world can quickly identify with Greek art, literature, philosophy, sport, military arts, and sciences. As well as other significant aspects of Greek thought such as astronomy and mathematics; these arts above and sciences did not originate in Greece. There is ample evidence and testimony by acclaimed philosophers and historians of ancient Greece such as Herodotus in 500 BCE, Pythagoras, Plato and many others to support this fact. Many of them were put to death for the knowledge they imported into Greece. So significant was the source of Greek knowledge and culture, that the earliest inhabitants of the land derived their very name Greece from an ancient name for Africa, *Nigrecia!*

The year was 776 B.C. at a time when Egypt was already ancient, that the Greeks began the practice of wrestling in honor of the African God Amon, whom they renamed Zeus. The entire Greek pantheon of Gods and Goddesses are based on African deities that were just renamed. Despite all of this, however, it is significant to our study that Greece provides one of the first instances of a martial art and religious tradition being combined in the west. However, it was a tradition based on older African practices that the Greeks adopted, but never fully applied.

All present day scholars of what is commonly known as Greco-Roman wrestling attribute the origins of their sport to illustrations discovered on the walls of tombs, in a region of ancient Egypt called Mahez. Which has been renamed "Beni Hasan," or "hill of the son of the Hasan family." Although considered just a sport today, these illustrations point to a well-developed science that actually developed in Nubia but reached the zenith of expression in Egypt.

At Beni Hasan, in four separate graves, there are hundreds of paintings on limestone walls that, for the most part, have since decayed. The paintings are of African martial artists using a variety of wrestling holds and locks. The illustrations total well over 500 individual pairs of wrestlers who are executing hundreds of sophisticated techniques. These images are mainly recorded in the tombs of governors, or princes by the names of Baqet III, his son Khety, and his son Amenemhat. They all reigned in Mahez during the 11th and 12th Dynasties. Illustrations were also found in the well-known Tomb of Prince Khemenhotep. The paintings feature pairs of fighters who are wrestling, as well as pictures of warriors using other forms of unarmed combat that employ kicking and punching techniques. There are scenes of martial artists using weapons such as a lance, short sticks, daggers, staffs, and bow and arrows. There are even scenes of warriors utilizing military technology such as a Testudo, which is a shielding device used during the siege of a castle. The earliest representation of a castle in the world can be found illustrated on an incense holder that originates from Nubia, the "mother civilization" of Egypt. Several paintings of castles in the Mahez tombs predate what we believe about the birth of castles, fortifications and medieval technology from Europe's Middle Ages. All total, these paintings in Africa represent the most ancient, and prolific depiction of martial arts on Earth.

Besides the accounts of ancient Greek historians themselves, information confirming the Greek's access to Egyptian arts and sciences were recorded by 17th and 18th century Europeans, those that were in Egypt such as Edme F. Jomard, James Burton, Jean Champollion, Robert Hay, and others. The most complete and often referred to the archeological study of the Mahez tombs were compiled by the Englishman Percy Newberry. Working for the Archaeological Survey of Egypt between 1890 and 1892, Newberry carried out "excavations" at Beni Hasan. The results were published in a two-volume work, as the First and Second Memoirs of the ASE (Percy E. Newberry, Beni Hasan), Part I [London, 1893] and Beni Hasan, Part II [London, 1893]. He states that graffiti on the walls that were written in Greek further proves that the Greeks were frequent visitors to the tombs in ancient times.

During the European colonial expansion and the advent of the Atlantic slave trade, Africans could never be credited with the development of martial arts. While Europe was so-called "excavating" icons, treasures, as well as people from the African continent, they were also hard at work covering up Africa's contributions to the world, and instead promoted the notion of African inferiority.

The modern interpretation of the martial arts owe their origins to the African martial arts tradition and can be found in the histories of the aboriginal Ainu of Japan, the etymology of the word karate, along with the history of the Buddha, to name a few, for example. Buddha's background and principles of thought can be traced to the Black people in India known as Dravidians. They inherited India's older Black civilization known as the Harappan civilization, which existed from around 4,000 BCE and was the contemporary of Nubia prior to the first Egyptian dynasty. In the centuries that followed, the Dravidians of India experienced a cultural and religious invasion from the north (circa 1,500 B.C.) by Indo-Europeans who called themselves Aryans. After centuries of conflict as recorded in the epic Mahabharata, the Aryans prevailed. They absorbed much of the arts, sciences, and religious deities of the indigenous Indian population and in its place, established the caste based faith of Hinduism.

In 520 A.D., a monk named Bodhi Dharma left southern India for China to re-define and spread the teachings of the counter religion to Hinduism called Buddhism. Buddhism was a religion founded on the teachings of Siddhartha Gautama who taught the Four Noble Truths to enlightenment. While often portrayed as Asian, the Buddha was a Black man. Sir Godfrey Higgins, an 18th century English scholar of ancient culture, produced a two-volume work published in 1836 titled *Anacalypsis; An Inquiry into the Origins of Languages, Nations, and Religions.* His research reveals in the following passage that, "In the most ancient temples scattered throughout Asia. Where his worship is yet continued, he is found black as jet, with the flat face, thick lips, and curly hair of the Negro." Today we awake to the facts that Buddha's tightly curled knots of hair and elongated ear lobes are unmistakable African cultural traditions. They are not "snails" that protect his holiness from the rays of the sun. Nor are his extended ear lobes "a sign of wisdom," as some scholars and early martial arts instructors used to teach.

At a temple known as Shaolin in China, Bodhi Dharma prescribed a set of exercises and movements to keep the monks healthy and awake during meditation. These movements and breathing exercises became known as the 18 Hands of Lo Han. They formed the basis of Chinese Shaolin Kung Fu and later, Japanese karate. (although it must be noted that the indigenous Ainu on the island of present-day Hokkaido, Japan contributed significantly to the transmission of the martial arts to those islands). Buddhist philosophy, which is derived from ancient Kemet, maintained that the exercises and the self-defense skills were designed to preserve the body. This is true because once the body was preserved it could be mastered, and utilized to unlock the spiritual centers within, and provide a pathway towards the liberation of the soul without.

In modern times, similar paths to fulfillment and spiritual enlightenment have been traveled by well-known fighters, both in and out of temples, churches, or mosques. For example, if you study the lives of martial arts masters such as Ed Parker, Bruce Lee, Muhammad Ali, and George Forman, you will see that a spiritual quest has refocused their lives. Ed Parker and Bruce Lee became profoundly religious in the later years of their studies. Muhammad Ali embraced Islam, and George Forman became a minister. These are not mere coincidences. This is the inevitable direction every serious martial artist, will eventually have to take. They may follow different paths towards liberation, but they will all find themselves on the same road that was paved for them in Africa over 3,000 years before Christ.

Going back to the tombs at Mahez during the 11th and 12th Dynasties, the meduneter on the walls of the tombs reveal much about the religious and military backgrounds of the four leaders. Text that accompany Prince Amenemhat's tomb explains that he was known to the public by civic titles. Such civil titles as, "Regulator of the two thrones" (Governor), and "superintendent of the two pools of sport." His military title was "Chief Captain of the host of Mahez." Prince Amenemhat is recorded to have had a standing army of 600 well-trained warriors who were successful in many battles. He was a benevolent man and much loved by his people.

Perhaps Amenemhat most significant titles are his religious ones. They included "priest," "chief lector," and "regulator of rank or succession in the temple," It is astonishing to visualize an African martial arts master and priest such as Prince Amenemhat, conferring status in a temple centuries before such scenes appear in Asia. Today, modern martial artists achieve rank with a belt, students' progress from a white belt to a black belt which is seen as the height of mastery. Even then, there are several degrees of black belts a warrior earns as one moves up in rank. The earliest recorded practice of soldiers putting on a "belt" before a workout can be found in Africa. The first two paintings on the East wall of the tomb of Baqet III depict two fighters who ritualistically tie a belt around their waists before they square off to begin sparring. The hanging ends of the belt familiar with modern martial arts are clearly depicted here.

In our century, when the legendary Black Karate Federation™ (BKF™) warriors, Steve Muhammad, (formerly known as Steve Sanders), and

Donnie Williams, fought on the tournament circuit in the early 1970's. These black belt warriors were two of the fiercest competitors ever. Over the years, their growth through the martial arts has led them to become known by other titles, as was Amenemhat in 12th Dynasty Egypt.

Kenpo Grandmaster Donnie Williams, who was also known by his civic title as a "law enforcement officer," is currently teaching a form of discipline that he has termed "Christian Karate." Grandmaster Williams is known by the title of "Bishop" for a church he has founded and ministered to for the past 15 years.

Kenpo Grandmaster Steve Sanders, in addition to also having been known by his civic title of "law enforcement officer," has chosen the spiritual path of Islam and has taken the name Muhammad. Grandmaster Steve Muhammad delivers his martial arts instruction and discipline backed by the moral and spiritual principles of the Islamic faith. As instructors, both men have produced an impressive roster of champions and both exemplify the continuation of a tradition that goes back farther than recorded history. Consider as well the fact that the BKF™ patch and logo depicts a cobra. To the Africans in Egypt and the Indus Valley, the serpent symbolically represents the rising up of a latent spiritual force or power as expressed through the body.

In addition to traditions, the African origins of the martial arts and the way they transform lives can be found in the very "names," of some of the disciplines themselves, such as "Pankration" and "Karate." As modern day martial artists, you may have been taught that in the Japanese language, *Karate-Do* translates to mean "empty hand way." *Kara* means "empty," and *te* translates to mean "hand." The word *Do* (in Chinese it is *dow* or *tao*) means "way." This is correct. However, let us look at a far older use for this term karate. When you break the word karate down, you get the most ancient Egyptian words of *ka, ra,* and *te.*

Ka in the ancient Kemetic or Egyptian language has a double meaning dealing with the spiritual, and the physical. Ka in the Kemetic language means the "vital energy of the soul," or the "man." The Ka is often described simply as a "body double" which does not convey it's understanding as soul or subtle vital energy. The Egyptian idea of a vital energy, Ka, is very much like *li* in Japanese, and *chi* in Chinese. Another definition of Ka in the Kemetic language is "body," or more precisely, "the dead, or empty body," as in the mummy.

Ra, or *res* in the Kemetic language, means "to wake up," "to rise up," "to keep awake," or "to watch." Ra is also the name that was given to the Sun (as in the Egyptian Sun God Ra) which renews itself by circling to re-appear. In fact, you can find the prefix *re* in many words in the English dictionary that point to their Kemetic origins. "Why would Egyptian words show up in the English language?" you may wonder. This is because the early settlers of a European land revered the African/Egyptian symbol of the cross known as the "Ankh." They named their land "Ankh land," which over time became "England."

Te or *t* in the Kemetic language means hand. In the ancient Kemetic writing system the symbol for *Te* is "t" which means "out of, to go out; to emit; to give; to set; to place." Do not overlook the fact that the meduneter, (otherwise known as hieroglyphs, a Greek term meaning "writings of the Gods"), for *te* is an illustration of a hand. In Japanese the word *te* is also their word for hand.

The most compelling evidence for the direct interaction between Egypt and Japan are found in a wonderfully detailed painting on the walls of the tomb of Prince Khemenhotep II from the 12th Dynasty. It depicts a group who were known as the Aamu. Eight men, four women, and three children are portrayed. They are led by the royal scribe Neferhotep, who is holding a papyrus roll that announces a total of 37 Aamu, who are bringing kohl or eye paint as a tribute to Prince Khemenhotep II. The Aamu is described as Asiatic. They are light complexioned people, wearing clothes of bright patterns of colors. The men are all heavily bearded. These Aamu visitors are not depicted as bound captives, but instead carry weapons such as the bow and arrow, throwing sticks, and clubs. The Aamu is the ancient ancestors of the indigenous people of modern Japan known as the Ainu.

In the language of the Ainu, their name means "human." In their daily lives, they prayed to and performed various ceremonies to the gods whom they call *kamuy* (the ancient Egyptians referred to themselves as *kamau*). The Ainu aboriginals of Japan are heavily bearded and have thick wavy hair. Their brightly colored clothes are almost identical in pattern to the clothes worn by the Aamu in ancient Egypt. The language of the modern Ainu reveals further connections to Kemet. The Ainu word *reka* means "to raise livestock." The word *resu* means "to raise a child." Words like *rik* and *riki* mean "to go up," "to ascend," and "high." We have already explored the Egyptian term and concept *Ra, re* and *res.* The Ainu word *tek* means "hand." Also, worthy of note is the Ainu word *yukara* (yu-ka-ra) which originally meant "to imitate" or "to mimic." The yukara was said to represent epic poems believed to be the voice of the gods who were describing their own ceremonies. The Ainu always told these yukara in the first person and would always end with the words "so said the god."

As we understand the term *karate-Do* in the modern sense to mean "empty hand way." In the original Kemetic language the words *ka, ra* and *te,* along with the existing philosophies of Maat. Along with the process of raising the kundalini, translates more accurately to reflect the concept of the liberation of the spirit from the body. For the ancient Egyptians, this led to enlightenment and resurrection. The Greeks, whom we know studied these arts and sciences in Egypt. Named their martial art "Pankration" (pan-kra-tion) which they define as *pan,* meaning "all" and *krat* (ka-r-t) meaning "powers."

A more accurate definition I have arrived at regarding the term *karate.* Is that karate in the original sense of the word means, "the way to bring forth, or draw out the power, or essence of the spirit." The ancient Egyptians knew that the spiritual body was much more powerful than the limited physical body. Their entire society and culture were devoted to the pursuit of knowledge and spiritual enlightenment. Could it be that like yoga, the study and movements of the martial arts were originally intended to be used as keys to unlock the latent potential within us so that the spirit could rise up? If so, the few hundred years of modern martial arts practice that is marked by crass commercialism, may have very little to do with a tradition that is many thousands of years older. It could mean that the martial arts today are indeed not being practiced for the purpose they were intended.

Which further supports a spiritual agenda for the practice of ka-ra-te. The fact that in the ancient Kemetic language, ka-ra-te, not surprisingly, can also be written with the same meaning as *ka-rast* (ka-res-t), or "Christ." Which means the anointed one or the "risen." Did Jesus' spirit not rise up, from a dead body to become the Christ? Is this not what we call the *res*-u-rection, or rising from the dead? Stop and think.

Look at the reference to Jacob in Genesis 32:22. It is a reference to the martial arts! Jacob wrestled (w-*res-t*-led) with a man (his lower nature). He fought with this man for one full day. Jacob "rose up" and was victorious. He reached the place called *pine-al,* (the symbolic "Third Eye" of wisdom). He changed his name from Jacob to Israel to reflect his complete "in"-sight to the Kemetic principles represented by the female principle Isis (Is). The male principle Ra (Ra) and the divine El (El is the Hebrew word for God).

For Jesus, whom many believe studied in Egypt during his "lost years." It is not difficult to imagine him as a skilled spiritual warrior, a martial artist on his way to self-mastery to becoming the Risen, the Christ. The life of Jesus parallels that of another crucified savior and resembles closely in words and deeds. He is a dark Black figure whose name literally means "The Black One." I am speaking of the Black (not powder blue) warrior from India, who became deified. His colorful life and epic battles against the invading Aryans are recorded in the Bhagavad Gita. He is none other than the illuminated master, Krishna.

Every era produces ascended masters such as Krishna or benevolent warrior priests such as Prince Amenemhat of ancient Kemet. It is almost certain that during our modern era, the martial sciences in the West will lead a few practitioners if not more, to similar levels of insight and achievement. In Africa today, despite her many problems, there can still be found masters and warrior priests of high spiritual orders among the Dogon of Mali, the Ife of Nigeria, the Zulu of South Africa, and other African people. Traditional martial arts are still being practiced.

The Mesakin and Kao Nuba people of present day Sudan still have a mandate that requires every young man to enter into martial arts training. These arts have much more to do with the development and continuation of a spiritual tradition than anything else. Iowa State wrestling Coach Bobby Douglas, who claims direct lineage to the Nuba of Sudan, confirmed in a recent interview that, "Even today, wrestling is still a part of the religion (re-ligion) of the Nuba."

As humanity evolves from an age of belief and speculation, to embrace a future that demands knowledge and application, the most fortunate inheritors of these glorious arts will be the generations to come. From among their ranks, we may find martial artists, who will dare to rise above the philosophical and ego based approach, to the study of the martial arts. But instead get an understanding and apply the sciences as they were formulated in Africa many centuries ago.

To prepare for this, however, one must be ready and willing to take up this challenge, like that spiritual warrior Jacob. We must prepare to wrestle with and overcome our most formidable opponent ourselves.

The words of wisdom from the ancient African Tehuti that are found in The Kybalion are more important today than ever before.

What is Kumite?

From Wikipedia, the free encyclopedia
Kumite (組手) literally translated means "grappling hands" and is one of the three main sections of karate training, along with Kata and Kihon. Kumite is the part of karate in which a person trains against an adversary, using the techniques learned from the Kihon and Kata.

Kumite can be used to develop a particular technique or a skill (e.g. effectively judging and adjusting one's distance from one's opponent) or it can be done in competition.

Gohon Kumite and Jiyu Kumite

Since the word *Kumite* refers to forms of sparring, it covers a vast range of activities. In traditional Shotokan karate, the first type of Kumite for beginners is Gohon Kumite. The defender steps back each time, blocking the attacks and performing a counterattack after the last block. This activity looks nothing like the jiyu kumite (or "free sparring") practiced by more advanced practitioners, which is far closer to how karate would look if used in a real fight, especially because it is not choreographed. karate and other forms of martial arts have various other types of Kumite (e.g. 3-step, 1-step, semifree, etc.) which span this large range in

Types of Kumite

- Ippon kumite—one step sparring, typically used for self-defense drills
- Sanbon kumite—three step sparring, typically used to develop speed, strength, and technique

- Kiso kumite—structured sparring drawn from a kata
- Jiyu kumite—free sparring

Delivering Strikes

Many schools feel it is important that karateka "pull their punches." Karate training is designed to give its practitioners the ability to deliver devastating power through techniques like punches and kicks. Often the  aim of training is that each single strike should be enough to subdue the opponent. However, this clearly would make it difficult to train due to the possibility of injury. Many beginners, while sparring, will be instructed to develop control and accuracy first, then speed and power later. In doing this, it may seem like the student is pulling his punches, when actually, he is developing technique first. For injury purposes, certain targets are discouraged, like strikes to the knee and face contact for low ranks. Many schools prohibit strikes to the groin while others allow it completely. Some schools might limit contact to light contact all around while others may employ power usage based on rank.

Some karate schools focus more on sparring whilst wearing protective gear so that strikes can be delivered with their full power. Most karate clubs and most styles of karate make use of some sparring with control and some sparring with protective gear (from just gloves and feet gear up to full head and even chest guards such as with taekwondo). Even in full contact karate, punches are often "pulled" to some slight extent in training to minimize the occurrence of injuries that would interrupt practice for the participating students, but usually that will depend on rank, age, gender, and school. Nevertheless, it is believed by many that practicing either type of sparring allows the martial artist to develop both control and experience in delivering powerful strikes against an opponent. However, many practitioners of full contact karate believe that full contact/ full force strikes and kicks should be employed as much as possible because they believe that "pulling" the strikes can have a negative effect on the striking power of the karate practitioner.

However, a few more traditional clubs that never use protective gear for sparring (except groin and mouth guards that protect against accidental injuries) argue that a karateka will not be able to make their most powerful strike when sparring in the dojo (against a friend whom they no doubt do not want to injure) even if this opponent is wearing protective clothing. Therefore, the karateka will still be using some level of control, as is obviously necessary, and cannot truly capture the spirit of one lethal strike whilst sparring. Except for a life or death self-defense situation, the spirit and power of the single lethal strike can only be achieved when a karateka does not have to avoid injuring their training partner. The traditionalists, therefore, argue that there is no benefit to sparring with more forceful strikes.

However in Kyokushin Karate no padding [1] is used and fighters don't "pull their punches" as fights are finished by knockout.

Mixed Martial Arts

Source: Wikipedia, the free encyclopedia:

Mixed martial arts (MMA) is a full-contact combat sport that allows the use of both striking and grappling techniques, both standing and on the ground, from a variety of other combat sports and martial arts. Various mixed style contests took place throughout Europe, Japan, and the Pacific Rim during the early 1900s. In 1980, CV Productions, Inc. created the first regulated MMA league in the United States named Super Fighters, sanctioning ten tournaments in Pennsylvania.

Pennsylvania State Senate passed a bill in 1983 that prohibited the sport.[1][2] The combat sport of Vale Tudo that had developed in Brazil from the 1920s was brought to the United States by the Gracie family in 1993 with the founding of the Ultimate Fighting Championship (UFC).[3]

The more dangerous Vale-Tudo-style bouts of the early UFCs were made safer with the implementation of additional rules, leading to the popular regulated form of MMA seen today. Originally promoted as a competition with the intention of finding the most effective martial arts for real unarmed combat situations, competitors were pitted against one another with few rules.[4] Later, fighters employed multiple martial arts into their style while promoters adopted additional rules aimed at increasing safety for competitors and to promote mainstream acceptance of the sport.[5] The first documented use of the name mixed martial arts was in a review of UFC 1 by television critic Howard Rosenberg, in 1993.[6] The term gained popularity when the website newfullcontact.com, then one of the biggest covering the sport, hosted and reprinted the article.

The question on who actually coined the name is a question still in debate.[8] Following these changes, the sport has seen increased popularity with a pay-per-view business that rivals boxing and professional wrestling.[9]

UFC is a sport that brings together the world's most talented Mixed Martial Arts (MMA) athletes. The UFC was created in 1993 as a made for pay-per-view spectacle to garner worldwide attention. There never was a plan to proceed beyond one or two shows. The idea was to bring together champions of various martial arts and Olympic sports. Such as karate, jiu-jitsu, boxing, kickboxing, wrestling, sumo and other disciplines to determine which style would be most successful in the tournament. International support for the event was enormous. What began as a mere spectacle was transformed into one of the world's most entertaining sports events. Over the course of its eight-year existence and 31 events, the UFC has become the premier mixed martial arts event in the world, featuring competitors of multiple disciplines in a quest to become the ultimate fighting champion.

Facts and Figures

Established with the goal of introducing light to medium point Kumite to the major leagues, the Pro Teams KumiteSport Martial Arts League is poised to expand globally as it pushes for the professionalization of the sport. The Pro Teams KumiteSport Martial Arts is the most inclusive of martial artists, compared to other martial arts platforms, welcoming all interested competitors, both male and female, aged 18 to 50 years old. We are not putting an 18+ requirement on tournaments. In fact, a national tournament will start with ages 4 on up. However, the 18+ black belt winners will make up the team to represent that city/ state within the league. The National competition is based on the ancient practice of the Kumite or sparring, which has allowed martial artists since the ancient times to hone their skills through one-on-one combat. Each team participating in the competition must have 15 members with 2 of the members having management positions and the rest engaging as competitors. Thirty-two (32) organizations comprise the Pro Teams KumiteSport Martial Arts and it is open to all martial artists willing to compete in a light-to-medium contact point sparring League, the first professional sports league of its kind.

Martial Arts Statistics from Simmons Market Research:

- Approximately 18.1 million Americans participated in karate or some other form of martial art at least once in the past year. That includes 9.4 million adults, 5.5 million teenagers, and 3.2 million kids.

- 5% of adults say they participated in martial arts last year at least once, and a quarter of those (28%) say they do martial arts "every chance they get." This number is split 52% men to 48% and women.

- 63% of adults participating in martial arts are aged 18–34. 25% fall in the 35–49 age bracket, with only 11% being 50 years and older.

- 25% of all teenage boys and 22% of teen girls say they have participated in martial arts in the past year.

- Adults, who participate in martial arts, are more likely than non-participants to say that they enjoy taking risks.

- There are approximately 40,000 martial arts schools in the United States.

2 Formulating My Idea

The Beginning

I returned to martial arts competition and tournaments in 1997 when I was approaching 40. I returned to competition because I wanted to do something that was safe and would keep me fit. So I searched out to find Mike Genova. Mike Genova is my karate teacher. I earned my black belt from him and Keith Vitali in 1986. Genova Karate School was no longer located on Rosewood Drive; it was relocated to a new location off of Sparkleberry Drive, with a new sign, "Genova Family Karate." I visited the school for the first time since returning from Desert Storm (1991), sometime during 1997 when I walked in the school; Mr. Genova was surprised and happy to see me as always. We talked for a few minutes then I got dressed in my fighting gear and started working out. I would work out several evenings a week. Trying to get back into competition shape for up and coming tournaments. One night I went to Genova karate studio and was introduced to a young man by the name of Jimmy Sherman. Jimmy Sherman was a black belt in taekwondo and was teaching classes for Mr. Genova at the Sparkleberry location. I may not have mentioned that I was one of Mike Genova's students from 1976.

After I went into the military in 1977, I would visit the karate studio while on military leave and take whatever tests I needed to continue my progression through the ranks during my visits. In November of 1979, during one of my visits, I received my brown belt; my black belt was earned in 1986. I opened my first martial arts studio around Harlingen, Texas when I was living in McAllen, Texas.

My Brown Belt Certificate—Signed by Mike Genova

The last tournament, in which I competed, was Dewey Earwoods tournament at the Sheraton Inn; I retired from martial arts competition that Saturday. I was under a great deal of stress with my marriage and my career. So martial arts were no longer any fun for me at that time. I couldn't get into training, I was too stressed. I ended up not competing in that tournament in 2003.

This was when I made competitors aware of my concept with teams like in other major league sports. I mentioned to them about the possibilities from what I had seen in the movie, *The Best of the Best* when Korea was competing against the United States. During this film, James Earl Jones searched the country for the best martial arts talent, recruiting the nation's top fighters to compete against Korea. With some modifications, the same can be done with a light-medium point martial arts league.

On January 2, 2003, after running a few ads in the South Carolina States newspaper to employ ten individuals to help me start the Kumite Inc., the beginning of a professional martial arts league. I was able to get 6 individuals to meet with me at a restaurant to discuss the making of the Kumite Incorporated the company. I presented my concept for a professional martial arts league with teams to them. I required that they each sign a confidentiality agreement before I made the presentation which would be that of the Pro Sports Karate Association (PSKA). The objectives for 2003 were to create 11 karate teams. Hire approximately 18 personnel as the core organization. Purchase approximately 20 acres of land to be used for corporate headquarters and martial arts camps. Then take our karate show on the road, estimating 95 events for the first year. We documented the requirements to succeed; we acquired sponsors for all initial tryout locations, which ended up being sponsored by the Holiday Inn and Sheridan Inn hotels. The staff needed to create 4–12 teams would be approximately 16 personnel, and we would need league event locations. At that time, we had 11 professional karate team tryout areas provided free of charge by the Holiday Inn and Sheraton hotels. We had four events scheduled for January 11, 2003 requiring 16 personnel. We had two events planned for January 18th requiring 8 staff. Two events January 25, 2003 were requiring 8 staff, and in three events February 1, 2003 requiring 12 personnel. Our marketing team consisted of two staff. Phase 1 of 2003 was the following cities had been chosen for pro-karate team selection year one:

- For January 11 and 12, we had scheduled team tryouts for Weirton West Virginia, along with the Atlanta, Georgia Tigers, and the West Virginia, Weirton Cobras. We also had the Baltimore, Maryland Cranes, and the Gulfport, Mississippi Centipedes

- January 18 and 19th 2003, we had to go to West Chester, Pennsylvania for the Street Fighters, and to Columbia, South Carolina for the Mantis,

- On January 25, 26 2003, we had the Jacksonville, Florida Dragons, along with the Richmond, Virginia Scorpions,

- On February 1 and 2, we went to Totowa, for the New Jersey Assassins, along with the Triadelphia, West Virginia Lizards, and to Greensboro, North Carolina for the Warriors.

Personnel event requirements would consist of the following:
- The event manager
- an assistant event manager
- event operations and administration (timekeeper or registration)

As far as compensation, as a registered corporation in the state of South Carolina, we had, and still to this day have, 10 million shares of available stock. The offering made for employees that day was stated during the presentation. Each employee was given an opportunity to negotiate his or her annual salary. In return, they would sign an agreement, and receive a share certificate which was recorded and stored in the company safe. Expenses would be subtracted from revenue, deposited into the organization's bank account. Stocks would mature one year after the signed contract date. The value of their shares would be determined by their percentage of ownership and the total funds deposited in the company bank account.

Share Pool Dilution

Shares at the time were worth nothing. Through events and summer camps, the value would increase by depositing the difference from expenses into the organization bank account.

An Example

At the end of year one, if we as an organization have a hundred thousand dollars in our bank account, all shares would be worth one cent. Then you would multiply your share value. That's your return on investment. For example, say you have 50,000 shares, the near value at the end of year one would be $500. You then have the option to cash in your shares or work another year.

Agreement between you and the Kumite, Incorporated will be for one year, renewable at year end. That was the financial agreement offered by the Kumite Incorporated to hire employees. 10 million shares total were owned by the corporation. Event managers (part of the core organization) would subcontract: Judges, referees, etc. execute league events and oversee the entire process.

How We Planned to Make Money

Through Team Eliminations Events

- Registration fees of $75 for Kumite and $25 for each additional event

We were Offering Three Events

- Weapons
- Forms
- and Kumite

Martial Arts Summer Camps

- Daily pick up $150 per week
- Weekly pickup $250 per week
- Summer drop-off $350 per week

League Events

- 3–5 events a week

Kumite, Incorporated, leadership at the time included Dexter Kennedy, President, and sister-in-law, Marketing Director, Marshall and Marlvis E. Kennedy, Vice Presidents.

Team Tryout Criteria

- All events were black belt only events
- Eliminations were to be double-elimination
- Only first and second place competitors would receive awards
- First place winning competitor signs a one-year agreement to compete in the PTKMA 3–5 events per week depending on his/her team's schedule to the compensation agreement

Martial Arts Summer Camps

Immediately after the completion of the team tryouts, we would secure 20 acres of land and have a structure built to accommodate 250 overnight guests in what would be called the Kumite headquarters. In addition:

- The summer camp would be marketed during the league season
- The camps would be for children ages 6 to 17, and teach discipline, nutrition, self-defense, karate, jiu-jitsu, boxing, Muay Thai, and don't bully me principles
- 200 Participants with a daily drop-off rate of $150 per week equates to $360,000 in revenue during the summer

League Events

Based on 1500 spectators per event, and each team participating in two events per month through December 15, we expected to generate $2,137,500. The Kumite, Inc. was to receive 40% of the proceeds from each event, the winning team 35%, and the losing team 25%. Total revenue for 2003, if all objectives were met: $2,580,000 of which $1,297,500 would be in the Kumite bank account, making shares worth 0.12975 cents per share. Meaning 100,000 shares would be worth $12,975.

League Event Format

The two-hour format would consist of:

- Competitor introductions
- Team star, school of attendance, and other members
- Playing of the Star Spangled Banner
- Musical weapons
- Forms
- Rules announcement
- Matchup (one-on-one three 2 min. round Kumite)
- Team with the most points gets a win in the win column

League Participant Compensation

Competitor salary ranges at that time were based on six minutes of competition per event. Competitor event for forms and Kumite, compensation range, was $285 to $400, making an annual salary from $6285 to $8800. Team star pay would be 321 to 450 per event, making annual payment from $7062 to $9900. The compensation for Kumite, only competitors, would be $214-$300 per event, making the total compensation $4708-$6600. The conclusion statement of the presentation went like this:

The Kumite, Incorporated has designed a practical format, which provides an excellent opportunity for those interested in something different in martial arts, and most importantly a chance to make history. What are your questions?

That was the presentation I gave to the 10 members. I needed them to help me with the pro sport, karate team eliminations for 2003. We went to all 11 locations but, due to our lack of marketing and PR experience the events were unsuccessful. For this reason, we did not have a league in 2003. Eventually, I hired the six that showed up for the presentation and later added my brother, father, sister, and sister-in-law. I made sure they were all interested in taking sport martial arts to the next level. The next level being to create a professional league of teams starting with the 11 in which we had sponsors. Each of which shared sponsorship in the Holiday Inn and 11 city locations and logos added a website for the Professional Sports Karate Association (PSKA). My team traveled to West Chester, Pennsylvania; Biloxi, Mississippi; Towson, Maryland; Atlanta, Georgia; Columbia, South Carolina, and several other locations. We were hoping to recruit enough brown/black belt talent to create the first ever professional martial arts league with franchise teams like other major league sports. The traffic from our website led us to believe that we had a lot of activity at these locations. We also received a call from RS Mitchell, a very well-known and respected martial arts teacher in the industry. Mr. Mitchell had an interest in owning a team in the Northern area of Maryland.

So I divided my company into groups and then sent them to the eleven locations we had scheduled for team tryouts. The most competitors to have shown up at any one location may have been five competitors at any one of the eleven sites with as few as one or two people. These trips were quite costly. I was funding these trips and the league totally out of pocket. I learned a great deal from this experience. So I went back to the drawing board, never forgetting the lessons I learned and what they had taught me. So I continued to hone my idea and concept for implementing a professional league for point martial artist. As the years went by, I continued to update, modify and further define my martial arts concept.

3 The Franchised Concept

Approximately, May 2009, I received an invitation to listen in on a webinar about franchising. The webinar was given by the Franchise Marketing and Development Group, which was being facilitated by a young man by the name of Andy Klie. I was very impressed by what I heard during the presentation. In fact, his presentation led me to believe that I could successfully franchise my concept. At the close of the webinar, I took down Mr. Klie's number and called him.

Our conversation was brief; I gave him a quick summary of my idea and concept, and I asked him if he would consider looking at the business plan I had put together before he made his decision. From his presentation, I learned and totally understood that he and his company only took on special projects. They took on projects that were exclusive in nature compared to the norm. So I asked that he at least take the time to read through my business plan. I knew he was very busy, but with a quick review, he could at least give me an idea of what steps he thought I should take. So, I emailed him my business plan for consideration. Approximately 1 week later, I received a call from Andy. He said I had an interesting concept and that he liked it. I was very excited and interested in moving forward. He told me what the cost would be to get started, and once he received the payment we could get started. It took me a few months to come up with the money, I took a big gamble. This gamble is one that you hear about in the news during the economy the way things are going that you shouldn't do. I closed out my 401(k) account from my work at Bank of America and used those funds as seed capital to support the franchising of the Pro Teams KumiteSport Martial Arts (PTKMA). What was initially franchised as the Kumite Fightclub has recently changed its name to Stand-Up Against Violence Everyone (S.A.V.E.) America or plug in your city martial arts franchise. Say for the city Los Angeles that would be "The S.A.V.E. Los Angeles" martial arts franchise.

I actually believe this is it for me, my last chance at greatness and my last chance at really doing something positive for America as a whole. But I did realize this was a huge risk! In fact, some would consider it a gamble. I feel very passionate about this venture and strongly in the concept and potential from what this sport has transitioned into along with the possibilities of this if marketed correctly. I envision mixed martial arts being the number one sport in America within the next 20 years. I think the Pro Teams KumiteSport Martial Arts (PTKMA) is the foundation of things to come, as well as the future of martial arts.

My Concept

A Professional Point Martial Arts League

Let's talk about my idea, my concept of a professional point martial arts league. As a former martial arts competitor and sports enthusiast, this is a platform in which I would have personally competed had it been available to me. In other words, if this venue were already in place I would devote my free time and efforts to training in hopes of securing a team position. So a lot of my rationale and thinking has to do with what I've experienced as an athlete in all sports collectively asking or answering the question why not martial arts. Here's a little statistical research to help one better understand the landscape, possibilities and opportunity, if you will open your eyes to the possibilities. There are over 40,000 martial arts schools and studios in the United States. There are more than 2,000 martial arts schools in California. Looking at the demographic of the United States and the 40,000 schools state to state. I identified the states with the most martial arts schools or studios. Using the NFL as a model, I decided to start with 32 states for 32 teams. These top 32 states across the United States will be the foundation for the 32 teams to make up the league like that of the NFL for martial arts. My concept also includes a league season like the other major leagues.

SPORTS LEAGUE SEASONS		
Sport	Start	End
Basketball	October	April
Football	September	February
Hockey	October	April
Baseball	April	October
The PTKMA	February	August

So, if I were to construct what I think would be the perfect league for martial arts, there are a few ways this could be done:

1. An Annual Tournament

One way would be to implement an annual team championship tournament. A tournament in which teams competed for a cash prize. So there would be one annual national competition. All teams would register or pre-register through a website. Teams would go to a regional location somewhere in their region of the United States. This championship might last a week. Teams would get eliminated. Maybe this would be a double elimination event. Champion teams from the various regions would go to the city/state of the regional winners and compete for championships for say the East Coast/ West Coast then the National Championship. In the end, you would have one team that wins the National Championship. Point martial arts competitors travel the world seeking tournaments with prize money. The more credible the tournament, the better the guarantee. Having reliable sponsors would also be a benefit in ensuring prize money to winners. A tournament of this magnitude would have the possibility of being seen on TV or pictured in a top rated magazine. Yes, it costs a lot to travel. Starting with state or regional tournaments and the top team from each state/region goes to the nationals. That way we have a smaller national competition (and it costs the teams less money to compete in the smaller regional/state tournaments, meaning more participants). Lowering the cost of the lower levels of the bracket will mean more people fight.

2. Major Tournaments

We recruit the top tournament promoters, experienced and successful in hosting tournaments from within the 32 states. Give them an opportunity to make their annual competition the teams try out location for that state's professional martial arts team. After which teams would compete in their geographical divisions to determine division champions and on to a National Championship series.

3. Franchise

Sell franchise units. Open the doors for anyone with the capital to purchase the professional martial arts team franchise for their state and allow that owner territorial rights. Assist with interviews to hire the staff needed so the owner can be the owner and responsible for the financial aspects of the business. The franchisee would be responsible for having an annual tournament to determine the best of the best in that state to represent the state, and perform as the team. Rules and regulations for the league are listed later in the book. Owners would need to secure a building which make franchise cost higher if owners decide to own their building versus lease. Franchise costs would be reduced for owners that choose to rent and sign rental agreements. The specifics are listed under the franchise details. I think we've thought of everything, but you be the judge.

4. Implement a Draft

Identify 32 team owners. After identifying thirty-two owners, and they identifying their management staff i.e. coach and trainer we would implement a draft lottery. We would have a website where competitors, which are black belts ages, 18+ registers for the draft. The team owners and along with their staff would be given access to a back panel access to the website maybe a month prior to the scheduled draft to research the registered competitors. Each team owner would be required to draw a number from a bucket of numbers to determine their draft position for player selection. The competitors would be listed on the site and the team owners would pick team members in order from the numbers retrieved from the draft buckets until they've completely fielded their teams. Of course, the salary or compensation would be at a rate that would satisfy competitors to participate and enter into a draft lottery. Without credible sponsors, a draft would not be a future state possibility. Unfortunately, a professional point martial arts league is a new concept that hasn't been truly vetted or agreed to by the masses but a draft has the potential for the future in a professional point league. These are decisions that will be voted on and decided by team owners. At first, the league would only consist of competitors that are within the state or territory purchased by the owner for his/her team.

We realize that at first without some kind of draft system there would be some regions with a larger talent pool than others, based simply on population. The major sports leagues all have drafts where the "athletes" chosen can come from any state or even other countries and play for that team. The league has already determined the standard sized team will include 13 competitive positions and 2 management positions. A draft is a future state possibility as the concept and leagues' marketing grows and the target market has expanded.

As stated earlier, this is a new concept. Never introduced, new and fresh but once we get industry buy-in, I think within five years you can see the possibility of a draft with salary ranges worthwhile for competitors to relocate. Like employees do when they relocate for jobs yet still not making millions.

OK, why a team, you might ask. Well, when I think of most major league sports, they have teams. Family and friends tend to rally around a team. The games that I would consider major league sports would be the NFL, the National Basketball Association and the National Hockey League and Major League Baseball. All have team members with positions. Have you ever noticed how people have a tendency to follow teams, team members, and/or team players on teams? They end up rallying behind a particular athlete. That athlete gets fans. Wherever that individual goes, say whichever team drafts him those fans support that player and the team benefits because he now plays for that team.

I personally feel there is also an opportunity to do the same thing with martial arts. OK, so why am I focusing this league, specifically on 'point martial arts'? I see sport martial arts as a missed opportunity. For over 70 years here in America, point martial arts has been practiced with an increase due to the Bruce Lee explosion. I define sport martial arts as any martial art style that use safety equipment, and scores points making light to medium contact either by kicking or use of hand techniques to vital areas of the body. So there are some organizations, in fact, there are over 500 amateur tournament circuits here in the United States that at any given time may have 500 champions. Each amateur circuit may have its own champion for each weight class in Kumite (one-on-one fighting or sparring) and age group or classification for kata or forms.

This is what I'm trying to convey: Because of the culture set by baseball, basketball, and football, when kids start elementary school they can choose to play T-ball. When they go to middle school or elementary school, they may have the opportunity to try out for football or baseball. If they make the team they get the chance to play for the team. Then they go on to high school. After high school get a chance to play college sports and from college, they end up with the opportunity to get drafted into the Pros. So the NFL is no doubt the best marketing for football, period.

How do we build something so positive that can have the same impact the NFL has for football? How about a professional point league for martial arts? First, we need to define what the team would consist of, as far as competitors. How many competitors per team, how will they be categorized i.e. weight class, gender, etc....

Through the concept, I'm proposing, and I wish to implement, "teams" would not be loose groupings of individuals. They would work as a team and to do their best to get the most points. There would be actual teams facing off against each other, in point Kumite thirteen versus thirteen. Having been a point martial arts competitor myself. Retiring in 2003 after seven-plus years as an active competitor in the NBL and NASKA circuits. For this reason, I feel I have a good understanding of the current state of sport martial arts in America. Adding the new twist from my Total Martial Arts Concept can change martial arts the game (point). What I've done are researched a few tournament circuits. Took the black belt weight divisions used in numerous martial arts tournament circuits to define what would make up a team. It makes logical sense from my research that you would be unsuccessful in having a black belt only event initially, at least until the concept caught on. I would not recommend having a black belt only type event; you would lose too much of the revenue needed to sustain the league. By, not including the other divisions and categories in your event, you would lose out on a lot of income. To be successful, we will also need commentators, and yes they will be necessary almost immediately at implementation. Commentators like the professional sports leagues have that are knowledgeable about the industry of sport martial arts. Commentators that can narrate the action, describe what is going on and the significance. This is one small piece of making the Total Martial Arts Concept a reality. This is just one of the opportunities that will keep former participants involved and give them an opportunity to stay in touch with the martial arts. It may take a little time for the concept to catch on. That is one reason for this book. Also, it may take time for the sport to grow in its popularity before a promoter could indeed benefit from a black belt only event. The competition numbers just aren't there for a promoter to benefit financially from a black belt only event.

My research tells me the team eliminations would have to be a complete tournament one that has all the divisions that are standard in major tournaments across America…ex. Kumite, grappling, forms etc.… from ages four up to sixty along with all of the groups and categories. So at present we are looking at possibly 32 major annual tournaments from within 32 states.

My goal is to find 32 team owners. But first let's get back to the annual competition itself. This annual event will determine the best of the best in that state to represent that state or city in the national championship of the Kumite Sports Championships. So we are just making the team from the annual tournament, using that annual competition's 13 best competitors. Those that win 1st place in the black belt Kumite (fighting) divisions would be the team to represent that city/state against the other 31 teams for the national championship. That's correct; each of the 32 teams would consist of 13 competitors.

Maybe I haven't made my point clear as to why I chose point martial arts, instead of what we see on TV and pay per view as Mixed Martial Arts (MMA). I consider MMA to be a more extreme martial art due to the rules of play. Or you may ask why I wasn't more concrete and select

Taekwondo or Hwarangdo? Well, the reason why I chose point martial arts if you noticed, first of all, I'm not doing this to downplay mixed martial arts...at all. Mixed martial art has evolved and there'll always be a place for mixed martial arts. I would categorize mixed martial arts as extreme martial arts. I noticed from tournaments like 'Battle of Atlanta', and some other tournaments...like the 'Mountain View Karate Tournament'. I see martial artists that participate in sport (point) tournaments, compete well into their 50s and up to 60 years of age. So there's an opportunity to have a team that would include the five divisions for the black belts, 18 and plus. Then there would be members 35 plus, and 45 plus; there'd also be females on the team and along with management positions: a coach and a manager. What this does, this sets up the opportunity, if you will, for martial artists. Once they've graduated or retired from competition, they could become a coach or a manager. The coach role could serve a dual purpose, a trainer and coach position.

So now when fighters have finished fighting and the teams have been determined through an annual tournament, these individuals will get a chance to represent their city/state for a year. In my opinion, this is the quickest way to grow the league concept. Most importantly, the revenue, that comes in from the registrations will be needed to finance the teams. Just imagine having your annual tournament as the team tryout event that determines the professional organization that represents your city/state in the national championships, and maybe that championship is called 'KumiteSport.'

OK, so KumiteSport will be the premier event for point martial arts where they have a consistent set of rules they follow; which will be light to medium contact. The champions that secured their team positions. People in those local communities are going to support them. As you have events in your region to determine the regional champion or division champion...it's like in baseball or basketball in the NFL, once those division winners have won and been determined. Then they will compete against the champions or first place winners from the other group to determine who the Northern, Southern, Eastern and Western Division champions will be.

I think one important question that everyone will ask is: How will competitors be compensated, right? Compensation, how will competitors get paid? So they're a couple of ways this can be done. There are ways in which competitors can get paid once they have secured their team position.

They Can Get Paid

- By getting a percentage of the revenue coming in the gate
- By getting paid a salary or
- By how well their team does in the division

This is something I haven't finalized or etched in stone yet because I would like the team owners to get an opportunity to weigh in on how they would like to compensate their competitors.

As far as building this enterprise I recommend we develop like Vince McMahon did with the World Wrestling Entertainment (WWE). The WWE created a fan base by holding events within the local communities throughout the United States by using high school gyms. When I attended high school and would get out of school for the day, I'd see signs of wrestling events that were coming to my high school. Maybe you remember. These were the school-sponsored wrestling events. There was an agreement with the school that involved schools and communities supporting the wrestling event that was to take place that evening or week at the high school. They're in my opinion lies the perfect strategy for us to grow and sell the concept.

For over 70 years in America, the sport martial arts have been growing strong but we've never put it on a platform for spectator entertainment. The Karate Kid movies helped a great deal but then the industry went back to full-contact karate with the boxing gloves and boxing techniques, and/ or tournaments with twenty plus rings going on simultaneously.

When you go to a tournament, a large tournament like the Battle of Atlanta or the Battle of Baltimore, there can be as many as 20 rings or 40 rings going on at the same time. So you end up walking around trying to figure out which event you want to watch. The best I've found, the best events of the evening are usually the night time finals. If I were to take a product to market, the night time finals would be it. That would be the part of a martial arts event. Where you get a chance to see all the champions, when the best of the tournament compete against one another, the best competitors in the game. That level of competition is so great and high, I think that's the opportunity. That's what we want to present to our public. We take that; put that into a 2–3 hour format for spectator enjoyment, and we have a goldmine. My selling point is we should consider the entertainment provided by our events and not at the knockout or how violent our sport can be or should be for the marketability to the few. Remember, we've made modifications to the traditional Kumite to make it sport-like. Now we can go one step further and make that a product package it and charge like they do for other entertainment venues such as theater, movies, and even plays. When was the last time you went to see a movie? It costs to see a movie and when you go a movie can last anywhere from 2–3 hours. For one person, I paid $8.50 to see a movie and if it was a 3D movie and I needed to get the glasses it could be another $5.00, but I get a military discount. So from having served in the military, I get a discount that saves me $1.50 to $2.00 per movie. Prices for those that weren't in the military or retired from the military can cost as much as $10.50; even seniors get comparable discounts to those that served in the military. So for 2 people that's $21.

My goal is to pay competitors, those that secure team positions. I think initially we won't have to pay them a great deal because those individuals currently that compete in point tournaments sit and wait for their event at a competition for hours before their division starts. They may pay anywhere from $35.00 to $65.00 to register for an event and compete. Then they sit around and wait all day. I know as a black belt, I might have gotten to the tournament at 8, 9 o'clock in the morning and not fight till like 4pm. If you are a martial artist and have ever fought in a karate tournament you, know what I mean. Getting weighed in at 9 o'clock and not fighting until 3 or 4pm depending how big the tournament is, then if I win my division. I can win cash and a trophy or just a 1st place award. If I win the top cash prize, which can be anywhere from $50.00 to $500.00 which is when the Grand Championship is won. If I go to a large tournament, that top prize can be as much as $1,000.00 plus Grand Champion prize money.

Just imagine 32 teams or better yet 32 team eliminations tournaments. Each providing 13 competitive positions and 2 management positions to form the professional point martial arts team for the city. With tournament registration fees being anywhere from $35-$75 depending on the decision made by team owners. Also, you will have individuals that will pay registration fees to compete that attended a martial arts school but are no longer affiliated with their school. You will also have competitors that have attended traditional schools or were taught at a recreation center. You will also have those that learned martial arts from a book or from a magazine. You may even have those that watched a video to earn their brown or black belt and afterward reached a certain level of comfort and may practice just to maintain. Then there are those that work out at home, those that execute kicks and technique in their spare time. Personally I haven't met too many martial artists that weren't doing their best to make ends meet. Then there are those practicing the martial arts for fitness, exercise or for the art itself. Once they've obtained their black belt, they're working out just to maintain or reach a certain level of proficiency, stay in shape or are a real martial artist at heart.

So, the vision given to me by God is in the opportunity to transition amateur point martial arts to a professional level competition. Along with the opportunity for compensation that can grow over time to be like that of our NFL counterparts, point martial arts competitors and/ or those that compete in martial arts as a sport. I don't think any point martial artists are getting compensated other than those competitors that win first place divisions for black belt at the tournament and the Grand Championship. It may be just the 1st place winners. Winning their divisions they award black belts cash and a trophy. So with the addition of a league, even if it were a semipro league. Winning your division and securing a team position. Getting the recognition for being the best in your state, because you competed in an elimination event of the best competitors in your state. Along with getting a contract to compete on the professional team to represent your city/state would have to have some credibility. Securing a team position could be the greatest thrill point martial arts can offer. Other than TV or being in a movie, what else is there? I can see this being one of those things that would quickly get a TV contract. In fact, I've already negotiated a deal for a TV contract; I just have to establish the league.

In the major professional leagues, the pedigree and skill of every player is known, this too can be done with martial arts. There are existing circuits from which these competitors would graduate, the amateurs which we can compare to college football if the comparison will help. The commentators for martial arts can talk about which tournament circuit(s) they championed or what martial arts studio, instructor they were trained by and their competition stats. With the history of the competitors or the fighters, they fought to secure their team position. The fan base can grow and learn what to expect from these competitors and know they were the cream of the crop for that city/state. There would have to be some credibility in securing the team position from beating the best within your state for that team position. One issue could be the best doesn't show up for the event. As the commentators talk the sport they will speak of the event and over time the best, will feel the need to compete because of how popular the game has gotten.

Benny the Jet fought in Japan and beat their best. So if this goes "big," there will be nothing to stop franchisees from bringing martial artist from China to compete in the league using our rules. Competitors from around the world are already competing in US tournament circuits such as the National Blackbelt League (NBL) and the North American Sport Karate Association (NASKA).

Fans support their heroes. Just as in high school, when you had the football stars well it's the same with the local martial arts school champions. Having a professional team for fans to support, will cause martial artists to train and martial arts school competitors to aspire to participate and secure team positions within that league. The league will allow spectators to follow and support their heroes like they do in college football for bowl games and later in the pro games. My concept, what I call the Pro Teams KumiteSport Martial Arts, is where franchise teams can be owned, operated and sold like other professional sports franchises (NFL, NBA, NHL and MLB). Any owner must clearly understand the concept of a league with teams for the league to grow and expand. This concept is an actual benefit and value add for any team owner. It only makes sense for them to have exclusive rights to the talent within their area (city and/or state). Through my concept, the owner would have to secure his/ her territory through a Franchise Agreement. I am offering one the opportunity to purchase one of the three franchises.

Strategic Fit

MMA events have only touched the tip of the iceberg with the first Ultimate Fighting Championships (UFC) held in 1993. Yet there are still over 50,000 martial arts schools in America that practice using points, semi-contact, and safety equipment. In addition, there are over

500 amateur circuits that follow similar rules within their tournaments along with 75 Million taekwondo practitioners who all practice using points, semi-contact, and safety equipment. The Pro Teams KumiteSport Martial Arts would like to professionalize where those untouched by the MMA platform participate. The point martial art is where that majority of martial artist engage. We would like to implement a league for those that compete in what is known in the industry as point martial arts. By allowing martial artist ages 18– 60 the opportunity to compete and secure thirteen team positions. Represent their city/state in a national championship like the Super Bowl by implementing a professional league with teams as it is done with other major league sports i.e. the NFL, MLB, and the NBA.

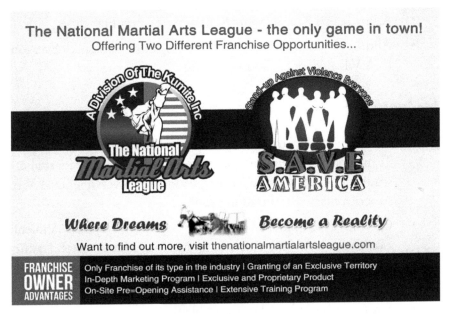

PTKMA Franchise Benefits Postcard

Our Target Market

Our franchise offering is for a Stand-Up Against Violence Everyone (S.A.V.E.) America Martial Arts School Franchise or a Pro Teams KumiteSport Martial Arts (Changed from NMAL to PTKMA [logo to be changed]) Team Franchise. The S.A.V.E. franchise has been specially designed for martial arts school owners that want to help their communities resolve America's top crime issues through martial arts education, training, and strategies. Opportunities are also available for those interested in owning that do not currently own a school or offer an annual tournament. Pro Teams KumiteSport Martial Arts Team Franchisees will be required to hold a significant annual competition for children ages 4 and up in all belt classes. The PTKMA Team Franchises will include teams comprised of the 1st place black belt division winners from their annual tournament(s) aged 18 and above. These individuals will represent their city or state depending on the level in which is purchased by the franchisee. The Pro Teams KumiteSport Martial Arts offers three franchise options based on the following two concepts:

- A Pro Teams KumiteSport Martial Arts Team Franchise
- And/or a stand-alone Stand-Up Against Violence Everyone (S.A.V.E.) America Training Facility

This Includes:

- Ownership of your own Pro Teams KumiteSport Martial Arts Team Franchise requires conversion of your existing martial arts studio, to a Stand-Up Against Violence Everyone (S.A.V.E.) America martial arts training facility.
- Or the development of a new Stand-Up Against Violence Everyone (S.A.V.E.) America Franchise. Martial Arts Training Facility with programs structured to combat relative top crime issues within the community it which it resides such as:
- Stress—America's #1 health problem
- Adult Obesity
- Crime—16% of US citizens will be victims of crime
- Bullying—90% of 4th–9th graders report being victims of bullying

Marketing Support for point martial arts which will bring needed recognition to the martial arts world and another platform choice for spectator entertainment for the masses; specialized community programs such as:

- Onsite self-defense for businesses

- Teen Scene—teen social network

- FightNITE—participants with a score to settle agree to fight with protective equipment, judges and in front of an audience for Friday/Saturday night events

In addition to voting rights to determine the organized, controlled scoring environment that will standardize the competition for martial artists of all styles. Ownership rights for the team tryouts, the products for your territory to secure a team that will compete against other teams in the PTKMA like in other major league sports.

PTKMA Franchise Options

The PTKMA is offering three franchise options to individuals and companies seeking to be part of the professionalization of a light-medium contact point league and help in our Nations Fight against crime.

These Include:

- A Stand-Up Against Violence Everyone (S.A.V.E.) America Franchise Martial Arts Studio

- the Pro Teams KumiteSport Martial Arts Franchise Team

- and the Master Franchise, which includes the two previously mentioned options plus selling rights of the Stand-Up Against Violence Everyone (S.A.V.E.) America Franchise to recoup franchise fees and get royalties

S.A.V.E. America

Stand Up Against Violence Everyone (S.A.V.E.) America is the martial arts franchise school of the Pro Teams KumiteSport Martial Arts, with the mission of "Making People Better for Life."

By providing programs to combat community issues such as:

- Stress—America's #1 Health Problem

- Adult obesity— More than two-thirds of U.S. adults are overweight or obese

- Crime—16% of US citizens will be victims of crime

- Bullying—90% of 4th through 9th graders report being victims of Bullying

A Stand Up Against Violence Everyone (S.A.V.E.) America martial arts training facility is focused and committed to supporting the mission by offering:

- On-site (at your work site or at their school location) certified personal instruction

- Providing focused health and fitness for children, teens, and adult obesity

- Offering education to women on how to fight back and regain control over domestic violence

- And teaching children and teens who feel threatened by bullies how to be empowered to take a stand and learn positive solutions to resolve conflicts

Stand Up Against Violence Everyone (S.A.V.E.) America will offer more than the traditional taekwondo martial arts program, currently being offered by the other schools in the area. Particular emphasis will be placed on the following programs and age groups:

- A value-priced White to Black Belt Certificate Program at $xx per month is expected to make up 22% of our membership with participants age(s) ranging 4–54 and a few from 55+.

- For children challenged by bullies, we offer positive solutions to resolving conflict by providing a Don't Bully Me Summer Camp Program. This is expected to make up 29% of our membership. The camp is hosted 10 weeks at $ per week during the summer for children age(s) 4–14.

- Teens ages 12 to 19 and young adults 20 to 24 experience the highest rates of violent crime. For them, we recommend our Take Charge—Self-Defense Program. This is expected to make up 35% of our membership with participants from the highest risk areas, a flat rate of $299 for either the twelve-week basic or advanced program.

- And for individuals with a BMI of 30 or greater. We offer the Build Your Dream Body Program, which we expect to make up 15% of our membership and are primarily for those that need supervision and guidance on how to exercise and train their bodies.

In addition, there is our National "S.A.V.E." Campaign in which Martial Arts School's that wear the logo participates. Those schools that wear the logo have agreed to a set of training standards and are focused and committed to tackling real community issues.

The Stand-Up Against Violence Everyone (S.A.V.E.) America or plug in your city is expanding Nationwide through franchising. S.A.V.E. America is the franchise name for our martial arts school franchise. Our franchise name just recently went through a name change and is now called 'The S.A.V.E. America Franchise,' which is an acronym for Stand-Up Against Violence, Everyone (S.A.V.E.) America. This is a ground-floor opportunity for existing studios to convert to a Stand-Up Against Violence Everyone (S.A.V.E.) America or plug in your city franchise or for entrepreneurs to establish a new martial arts school. Like most martial arts schools, Stand-Up Against Violence Everyone (S.A.V.E.) America or plug in your city martial arts franchises offer traditional structured white-to-black belt certificate programs. But, Stand-Up Against Violence Everyone (S.A.V.E.) America or plug in your city martial arts franchises also provide solution-based programs designed to resolve real community issues; including stress, domestic violence, bullying, and obesity.

The Don't Bully Me Program empowers children and teens who feel threatened by bullies to take a stand by learning positive solutions to resolve conflicts.

Other Programs Include:

- Onsite self-defense classes for businesses
- Courses that educate women on how to fight back and
- regain control over domestic violence
- Health and fitness solutions for child/teen/adult obesity; and a Teen social network called Teen Scene

The S.A.V.E. America or plug in your city martial arts franchise provides a place where people can learn the martial arts. Enjoy the experience of learning while making the commitment to study and improve their self-esteem, concentration, discipline, and self-control.

As students experience the programs, they gain knowledge and experience that last a lifetime. The martial arts industry is notorious for high membership turnover, with several reports placing the average attrition rate at 40 to 60 percent. The reason for the high turnover is because traditional martial arts facilities conduct business in a manner that is not conducive to the American way of continuous improvement.

Our remedy, to reduce the high attrition rate, is to offer specially-designed programs to fit each individual's specific needs.

These include:

- Effective self-defense programs offered in 12-week sessions for people needing only self-defense
- Fitness programs managed and monitored by a certified trainer for persons needing only to get fit

- Summer camps and weekend workshops for children that are being bullied
- Quality white-to-black belt martial arts training programs; and more, at fair and reasonable prices

This is an excellent opportunity for people who actually want to help people. The cost, to purchase and develop a new S.A.V.E. America or plug in your city martial arts franchise, can be as little as $57,400. The $57,400 franchise cost is based on purchasing the assets needed to sustain day-to-day school operations.

This may include:

- a building (lease or purchase)
- kick/punching bags
- and the other resources needed to maintain a full-scale school and have daily classes

Note: These costs are reduced tremendously for established schools.

This is a franchise option to set up and operate a school for martial arts. This option is open for a new business or to convert an existing martial arts studio into a training facility that conforms to the Stand-Up Against Violence Everyone (S.A.V.E.) America standards. Each authorized Stand-Up Against Violence Everyone (S.A.V.E.) America Franchise shall offer all services and products as detailed in the Franchise Agreement. The concept behind S.A.V.E. America is due to the rise in crime in America. We believe solutions can be created and implemented through specialized programs, some of which can be designed and created by martial arts masters and experts. There are individuals that when they come to a martial arts school just want to learn how to defend themselves solely and not have the time nor interested in completing a two-to-four year black belt program. A customer may have a 'bully' situation and want to learn how to defend against that bully, etc., etc. So instead of signing up for classes they sign up for a class specific to meet their need.

The value of a S.A.V.E. America franchise is that martial arts school programs are designed for the top 10 issues within that community in mind. We have capable staff available to assist in defining what those programs should be and require our school owners to offer those classes within their schools also to their traditional black belt program. Martial Arts School's that offer courses that provide a specific NEED will allow the school to be a value-add within the community. These schools operate within the city offering courses that have been designed for the school in that town to be successful as a martial arts franchise. So that adds value to the community because your franchise provides solutions within your community to resolve community issues through training and education within the community.

If a martial arts school starts running their own program, and that school replicates what S.A.V.E. franchises do, without paying the $57,400 or franchise fee. To do so and be effective, they must totally understand the vision and concept. If a school does adopt the S.A.V.E. concept without paying the $57,400 then both the community and martial arts benefit. The goal of the Total Martial Arts Concept will have been met. Solutions-based schools, martial arts schools with the community in mind, schools that offer programs that resolve known community issues. Which not only add value to the franchise but also allows the franchisee the opportunity to access grant dollars to grow his or her franchise school. In fact, grant dollars may be available for your initial purchase depending on the community and location. One benefit in owning is the PTKMA will evaluate your community and assist in determining the best programs for success. We promise there will be no competition within a 50-mile radius of one another. These fees below are based on a $400,000 a year school per our SBA approved martial arts school business plan.

Estimated Start-Up Costs: can be anywhere from$ 77,000.00 to $ 258,000.00

Note: There are also the costs for travel to Columbia, SC for a 5-day training program. This may be waived for experienced tournament promoters or school owners.

Initial franchise fee: $ 25,000.00 to $ 75,000.00 lump sum Royalties: a minimum fee of $ 1,000.00 per month or 6 % gross revenue, whichever is greater.

Marketing fund royalty: 3% of total revenues

Stand-Up Against Violence Everyone (S.A.V.E.) America Kids Programs

- White belt - black belt tiny tots program
- White belt - Black belt beginners program
- White belt - Black belt intermediate program
- White belt - Black belt advance program
- Fight Back - Self-Defense basics (certificate program)
- Fight Back - Self-Defense advanced (certificate program)
- The Teen Scene
- Don't Bully Me Program

Stand-Up Against Violence Everyone (S.A.V.E.) America Adult Programs

- Fight back - Self-Defense basics (certificate program)
- Fight back - Self-Defense advanced (certificate program)
- White belt - Black belt beginners program
- White belt - Black belt intermediate program
- White belt - Black belt advance program
- FightNITE
- Kata-Forms for Strength and Flexibility
- Build Your Dream Body 12-week program

The National S.A.V.E. America Campaign

Join us in our nationwide campaign to S.A.V.E. America, the National Stand-Up Against Violence Everyone (S.A.V.E.) America Campaign. The goal is to get cities across America to sign up and commit to one weekend a year where:

- The mayor
- City government
- Law enforcement
- Paramedics
- Local martial arts school owners
- School teachers
- Nurses

Come together, discuss and provide solutions to identified community issues. During the annual weekend, we will have meetings, conferences and workshops in which members of the city get together with city government. The group works as a team, takes a look at their city and determines solutions to the top 5 crime related issues which most likely will be any of the following:

- Violent crimes
- Rape
- Domestic violence
- Manslaughter
- Arson
- Bullying
- Property crimes
- Break-ins
- Theft
- Home invasions

The group will be split up into smaller groups by area, dissect their communities, identify issues and come up with solutions as part of the S.A.V.E. your City campaign. During that weekend, there will be meetings, conferences and workshops in which the city takes a look at their top crime related issues which most likely will be from the list of those recorded below.

Vendors will be able to Rent Booths for Sales:

- House alarms
- Self-defense weapons
- Self-defense videos
- Self-help workshops and videos/DVDs

There will be classes for students, women and children and all areas of violence for that weekend. Martial Arts Schools will run special promotions for their Bullying, self-defense, and rape prevention programs, etc....

Individuals, cities and businesses interested in joining the campaign please contact: dkennedy@thenationalmartialartsleague.com

Our Mission

The primary goal of S.A.V.E. America is to get as many states as possible involved. States interested in participating will need to choose a weekend in which they can totally focus on saving their city. During that week, the city will need to get the mayor, chief of police, first responders, national guard, teachers and school principals together to talk crime prevention. The entire community will need to get involved and conduct seminars, workshops and training on:

- Drugs
- Gang recruitment
- Self-defense

- Domestic violence
- Rape prevention
- Conflict resolution

Note: With vendors selling various products relative to those topics

The classes will be a requirement for martial arts schools to participate, for which they will be authorized to wear the S.A.V.E. America (their city) logo on their uniforms and/or their website. During the Stand up Against Violence Everyone (S.A.V.E.) campaign—we will be organizing communities with the goal of making the United States of America a better place to live, workand play. Various communities have been riddled with criminal activities, drug-related gangs, domestic violence, rape activities and corruption. Now it's time to take charge and get back our communities.

Objective

- To get individuals within communities involved in identifying solutions to minimize crime
- To bring about an improved way of thinking in individuals
- To improve community relationships and make them a better place to live

Operations

The campaign will be spearheaded by Dexter Kennedy. The chairperson will work with a team of persons from several backgrounds that will be able to organize and plan a successful campaign. This campaign will involve meetings with the mayor, chief of police, first responders, national guard, teachers and school principals in all states to talk about crime prevention.

Contact will be made with these persons informing them of our plans and obtaining a date that will be convenient to discuss a plan to move the S.A.V.E. campaign forward in their community and overall for the

Event. The campaign will involve the entire community through seminars, workshops, drug training, gang recruitment; as well as, self-defense, domestic violence, rape prevention, and conflict resolution. Vendors could sell various products related to those topics.

The martial arts can be used as a tool to bring about positive changes in our communities. Some advantages of getting involved in the SAVE program include:

- Learning self-defense
- Acquiring better health and wellness
- Living with less stress
- Increasing one's self-confidence
- Developing new skills
- Receiving a fun form of exercise
- Meeting friendly people
- Living in a positive and encouraging atmosphere

To be eligible to participate in the S.A.V.E. America campaign martial arts schools, the enrollee will be required to pay an annual fee of $99.

The following courses will be:

- A 12-week primary, and a 12-week advanced self-defense course at a rate, not to exceed $199

- Identify a city qualified domestic violence counselor to offer two weeks of awareness counseling in concert with the self-defense courses. These informative classes will add an additional $49 to each self-defense course

- Rape prevention—course will include the self-defense primary/ advanced courses along with one month of crime prevention scenarios unique to the vulnerability and defending from the mount position

Also participating, member's schools will be required to provide demonstrations of their required programs during the annual weekend S.A.V.E. America campaign for their city.

All participating member schools will be required to display the S.A.V.E. America campaign logo with uniforms, schools and places of business. Students involved in the programs will also be authorized to support the program by wearing the S.A.V.E. America logo on their uniforms.

Promotion of the campaign will be done through schools, community centers, churches, sports arenas, clubs, and bars. Posters will be given to all these entities which usually host a wide cross section of persons for various events. Consideration could also be given to publishing the information in the daily newspaper that has the most readerships in each State.

Conclusion

All martial arts schools that meet the requirements for participation will be given the opportunity to participate. Annual S.A.V.E. America campaign attendees will receive discounts for signing up for S.A.V.E. America specifically designed programs during the annual weekend event.

This campaign has the potential to have a positive effect on citizens of the US. Proper planning and organization of the various events and activities will result in a successful campaign.

S.A.V.E. Foundational Classes

Stand Up Against Violence Everyone (S.A.V.E.) America school franchises will offer the following programs for different ages and skill levels.

Class Name	Description
Early Morning Workout	5 am workout
Private Instruction	One-on-one instruction
12-Week Self-Defense Program Basic	12-week self-defense program that teaches practical applications to a myriad of street situations. Two sessions every 12 weeks
12-Week Self-Defense Program Advanced	12-week self-defense program that teaches practical applications to a myriad of street situations. Two sessions every 12 weeks
12-Week Build Your Dream Body Program	12-week certified trainer managed and monitored fitness, health and training program
Midnight Madness	Midnight workout for those looking for a midnight rush
Lunchtime Fitness	2 ea. thirty-minute lunchtime workouts for those wanting to workout during their lunch time
OSSDP	12-week on-site self-defense program at your workplace. Flexible two training days a week program
White Belt - Black Belt Beginners Program	Traditional white belt to black belt program
White Belt - Black Belt Intermediate Program	Traditional white belt to black belt program
White Belt - Black Belt Advanced Program	Primary white belt to black belt program
FightNite	Martial Arts Kumite for viewed entertainment
The Teen Scene	Entertainment night for teens

Competition and Buying Patterns

The nature of the business of a martial arts school is to offer a facility for martial arts training. Membership is everything and turnover (attrition) in the industry can be high. Several reports place the average turnover of a training facility at 40 to 60%.

The average training facility teaches a traditional martial arts program which is not conducive to the American way of continuous improvement. S.A.V.E. America's remedy for the 40 to 60% attrition rate is to offer specific custom programs. Such as an efficient self-defense program for those needing *only* self-defense. Fitness by way of the Body for Life program for those needing *only* to get fit, and lastly a Summer Camp program for children that are being bullied. This new format along with the future of a professional point league should change the dynamic tremendously and allow Stand Up Against Violence Everyone (S.A.V.E.) America to exceed the competition in reducing its attrition rate.

Pro Teams KumiteSport Martial Arts to become reality

Ownership of a Team Franchise

Ever dream of owning a professional sports team?

A Pro Teams KumiteSport Martial Arts Team Franchise is a true ground-floor opportunity!

Competitors of all martial arts styles will be given an opportunity to represent their city or state by securing a team position and competing for the National Championship—The Kumite Sport.

For over seventy years, martial artists have honed their skills in one-on-one combat in hopes of being the best of best, or becoming the next Chuck Norris or Bruce Lee. So far no one, including investors, has yet to reap the rewards this sport can generate when it breaks out of its current limitations.

The Pro Teams KumiteSport Martial Arts is Offering:

- A league comprised of thirty-two martial arts team franchises. Each supporting an S.A.V.E. America Martial Arts Training Facility and summer camp. An adult recreational training facility for those families who see this as a way of spending quality yet fun and disciplined time together

- A national sport that brings needed recognition to the martial arts industry plus another choice of spectator entertainment for the masses, and

- An organized, controlled scoring environment to standardize competition for martial artists of all styles

The PTKMA is poised to propel the exciting sport of point martial arts to a new level by bringing the fragmented martial arts industry into organized events culminating in city/state championships across the nation. It provides a controlled scoring environment to standardize competition for male and female martial artists, ages 18 and over. This is a genuine ground-floor opportunity in sports team franchising, franchises may be owned by an individual, partnership, corporation or existing martial arts school, and each franchise operates autonomously within the PTKMA. This is one of the most affordable franchises to own and operate in professional sports today. The PTKMA is making a powerful move toward professionalizing the sport into state and national level recognition. It offers the masses another venue choice for spectator entertainment. And it creates niche market advertising and sponsorship opportunities for corporations and franchises. Each team develops its own identity and owns team tryout rights for its defined and protected territory to secure team members, coaches, trainers, etc. The teams compete locally, regionally and nationally with other teams within the PTKMA, like other major league sports.

As a team owner, franchisees are required to support The Kumite's mission of 'making people better for life'. They must either establish a new Stand-Up Against Violence Everyone (S.A.V.E.) their city, state, or country martial arts studio. Or convert an existing school to a Stand-Up Against Violence Everyone (S.A.V.E.) their city martial arts instruction and training facility. The PTKMA recently conducted a full review of its business model And began molding new strategies to better serve the long-term success of the league and franchises. Each year of operation and success will enhance the overall team operation and add value to the teams and franchises."

A Pro Teams KumiteSport Martial Arts Team Franchise defines a protected territory in which ownership of a particular Pro Teams KumiteSport Martial Arts Franchise can be exercised. A team shall consist of black belts—martial artists of all styles, male or female, aged 18 and above. The area boundaries are determined by a number of factors including population, median population age, and proximity to other franchisees.

The PTKMA is currently seeking 32 team owners that can be either existing tournament promoters or individuals, partners or business persons interested in hosting annual events. These individuals will represent their city/state and use the first place 18+ black belt fighting competitors from their annual event to compete globally in a world martial arts league. The 32 teams will compete against one another for a national championship in the Kumite National Championships. This opportunity allows individual martial artists and teams to bring home more than trophies and medals. A Pro Teams KumiteSport Martial Arts Franchise Team offers instant recognition and guaranteed profit. The public is also provided with another option for spectator entertainment.

Note: Start-up costs and fees may be lowered by as much as 80% for owners of existing tournaments and or established martial arts training facilities.

When Pro Teams KumiteSport Martial Arts establishes itself as the first professional point martial arts organization utilizing the TEAM concept, it will set into motion an array of profit generating revenues. This TEAM concept to be guided by FAMILY-ORIENTED entertainment for domestic distribution and sale will support the spectator community with live event tours.

For many years, the various genre of the sport has languished within limitations of communities, independent training schools, and the occasional large events. Now the Pro Teams KumiteSport Martial Arts is making a powerful move toward professionalizing the sport into state-level recognition. The potential for a profitable investment is based on the very fertile ground of the majority of martial arts fans that range in ages 3 to 93. Are 40% female, and very active in the 21 to 49-year old male segment of the population. Pro Teams KumiteSport Martial Arts sees this vast neglected middle ground between kid's martial arts training and hardcore martial arts extreme. From this perspective, the Kumite, Inc. will uncover the nation's future lead martial arts organization for maximum profit potential to those who are heavily invested.

Products and Services

The Pro Teams KumiteSport Martial Arts will provide the first professional point martial arts league utilizing the state team concept. They will also support the S.A.V.E. America summer camp program where children will be taught positive solutions for today's problems using PTKMA superstars.

The largest majority of martial artists follow one of the amateur point circuits with no graduation other than a few full contact Mixed Martial Arts organizations such as the UFC for recognition. The Pro Teams KumiteSport Martial Arts will challenge the martial arts community, by waking up the martial arts community in providing the opportunity to secure professional team positions. By paying a small registration fee to compete against the best, their state has to offer to secure a team position in which they will be paid to represent their state competing in the National Team Championships.

Compensation and getting paid to fight will wake up martial artists everywhere. Start a training frenzy and allow us to reap the monetary benefits of all fallen by the waste side only to shell out purses for the finals. As the team concept catches on more competitors will come out of the woodwork allowing us to offer salaries and contracts by the close of year three.

The Pro Teams KumiteSport Martial Arts will establish itself as the first professional point martial arts organization utilizing the TEAM concept to offer quality FAMILY-ORIENTED entertainment for domestic distribution and sale. It will support the spectator community with live event tours. Additional revenues will be generated from:

- Weekly pay-per-view events
- Get Paid to Compete video sales
- S.A.V.E. America summer camps
- Team Franchise sales and memorabilia
- Onsite event tickets
- Merchandising of souvenirs, future magazine, concession items, live event video sales, etc.
- Future franchise sales (teams and summer camps)

While the top two professional martial arts organizations currently have a stronghold on the business. They are, for all intents purposes, mirror images of each other creating the same type of product that is limited in its nature and appeal. The PTKMA programming will always be family oriented and, thus, have great mass appeal, projecting the PTKMA into the #3 position within the industry within 3 years.

In addition to using established, well known martial arts stars including former ISKA, NASKA, and NBL stars, the PTKMA will develop its own stars of the future.

The Teams

I've already come up with 32 team names and logos; we've even identified the states with the most martial arts schools for team locations. Just to give you an idea of my concept, if the NFL crossed with Kung Fu Cinema and American Idol, you would have an understanding of the Pro Teams KumiteSport Martial Arts. I used that analogy because almost everyone thinks they can sing or at least a vast majority does. I think there's a vast majority of the population if taught could learn sport martial arts and compete. Let me remind you, I am solely talking about point martial arts. Not the more extreme martial arts. Extreme martial arts is different, it takes a different mindset and demeanor. Mixed Martial Artist (MMA), those that compete within venues like Strikeforce and UFC, tend to be more aggressive and on the edge. When they train, they train hard like professional boxers. They may find a boxing trainer and learn how to box. Take a few months of martial arts and learn a few kicking techniques grappling; judo or jiu-jitsu and they are ready for their first Mixed Martial Arts (MMA) match. That's not the case for most traditional martial artist. Sport (point) martial arts are actually less physically demanding primarily because of the rules, respect and honor that come along with the tradition making it an entirely different animal. There are spectators that would be entertained by a point martial arts league, and its tradition and the benefits and value it brings to the sport, competitor, and culture. So in my concept if an owner decides they want to purchase the state rights to a particular state, then they would have access to all of the participants within their territory for their team's annual tryouts.

Below you will see the team names I came up with. I love to watch martial arts movies. Such as the Five Fingers of Death, Five Deadly Venoms, Spearman of Death. The list goes on, the older, the better. Especially Shaw Brothers movies. Because of my love for the martial arts genre, as a tribute to that genre I decided to take t liberty and name the league team names and make them about the martial arts genre and martial arts cinema. Also, I am an old school martial artist. I got involved in martial arts because of Bruce Lee and what I saw of him in his movie Fists of Fury. Due to his accomplishments I think he is entitled to the credits given here. Although I named the teams from the Kung Fu cinema genre of martial arts, I still give credit to the roots of ancient martial arts, being from Africa. To stay true to its legacy and since there have been so many changes made to the martial arts styles, through training and from the updates. So the names, I came up with, are relative to the old martial arts cinema. The thirty-two Pro Teams KumiteSport Martial Arts team franchise names have already been determined. I'm going to spend a little time and share them with you. The team names you will see shortly, of which we've already gotten logos designed for and completed, and more specifically for those interested in owning a Pro Teams KumiteSport Martial Arts team franchise with territorial rights.

The 32 teams would be divided up like in the picture below. We divide the United States into quadrants and we have 8 teams in each quadrant which will be called divisions. So the 8 teams would compete within their quadrant to determine the first and second place teams within those quadrants. Then the first and second place teams from those quadrants would fight against the first and second place teams from the upper and the lower two quadrants to determine the East versus the West conference champions. Then we'd have the East versus the West to decide the national championship.

The Pro Teams KumiteSport Martial Arts

Pacific Division	Mid Western Division	Northeastern Division	Southeast Division
Washington	Texas	Michigan	Kentucky
Oregon	Oklahoma	New York	Tennessee
California	Kansas	Massachusetts	Virginia
Nevada	Louisiana	Connecticut	Maryland
Utah	Missouri	Pennsylvania	South Carolina
Arizona	Illinois	Ohio	North Carolina
New Mexico	Wisconsin	New Jersey	Florida
Colorado	Minnesota	Indiana	Georgia

Proposed Professional Point Team Locations
(Can be expanded worldwide)

PTKMA Team Names

The Golden Eagles	The Five Elders	Ten Tigers	Knights of Darkness
The Death Squad	The Street Fighters	The Golden Centipede	Thirty-Six Families
The Wou Kou Pirates	The 9 Dragons	7 Clans of Kung Fu	The Mantis
The Black Emperor Scorpions	The Shaolin Warriors	The White Crane	The Red Lotus
Snake Fist Fighters	The Eight Immortals	The Midnight Assassins	Komodo Lizards
The Five Animals	The Dragon Society	The Black Cobra	Forest Ghosts
The 36th Chamber	Shaolin White Snake	The Venom Squad	108 Locking Hands
Masters of the Eight Laws	The Red Fist Clan	The Iron Monkey	The Poison Clan

The Team Uniform

There are quite a few martial artists that will disagree with me. Mostly the old school martial artists will disagree with the implementation of a new professional point league, and the need for a uniform update. A new sports uniform, an update to the traditional martial arts uniform to a more trendy sports uniform. So I worked with a graphic designer to take what I envisioned to be a new updated look for professional martial arts sports competition. I looked at superheroes uniforms like Captain America, The Flash and even watched movies like GI Joe. After a few months of research, we came up with the uniform you see below:

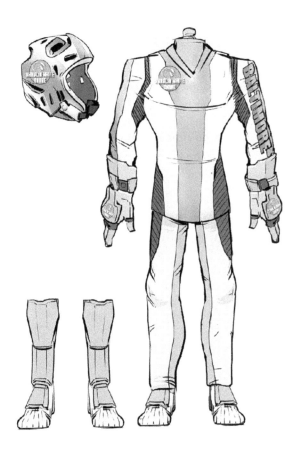

Proposal for PTKMA Uniform

Several Key Points I would Like to Make in Regards to the Uniform:

- The headgear is simply nothing more than the standard popular brand headgear seen worn at most martial arts tournaments. It's been colored to support the teams color scheme which is similar to the Pittsburg Steelers. The headgear also has the team logo affixed to it, in this case, the Shaolin White Snake

- The uniform color scheme is complimented throughout the entire outfit with the city embroidered on the left sleeve in this case Baltimore. The uniform also has the team logo embroidered on the upper right shoulder area affixed onto it, in this case, the Shaolin White Snake

- The shin guards, which will be worn under the uniform, are also fit the team color scheme

- The hand gear also goes with the team color scheme which is the popular brand super chop

Note: This popular brand supported us for our second team eliminations with sponsorship and is our primary candidate in having our team equipment design needs to be met.

Minor modifications to the Reksuit should allow us to have the uniform design of the future pro league, the Pro Teams KumiteSport Martial Arts.

The League

PACIFIC DIVISION	MID-WESTERN DIVISION	NORTHEASTERN DIVISION	SOUTHEAST DIVISION
WASHINGTON	TEXAS	MICHIGAN	KENTUCKY
OREGON	OKLAHOMA	NEW YORK	TENNESSEE
CALIFORNIA	KANSAS	MASSACHUSETTS	VIRGINIA
NEVADA	LOUISIANA	CONNECTICUIT	MARYLAND
UTAH	MISSOURI	PENNSYLVANIA	SOUTH CAROLINA
ARIZONA	ILLINOIS	OHIO	NORTH CAROLINA
NEW MEXICO	WISCONSIN	NEW JERSEY	FLORIDA
COLORADO	MINNESOTA	INDIANA	GEORGIA

PTKMA Proposed Teams & Divisions

League Competition Rules

For the purposes of this book, Martial Arts and Sport Martial Arts are interchangeable terms. Contestants may be referenced as martial artists, karateka, and martial arts competitor, Fighters, Competitors or Athletes. Officials and Referees are interchangeable terms.

Light-Medium Contact Martial Arts aka Sports Martial Arts:

- Takedowns, ground control, submissions and body strikes are not allowed
- Potentially dangerous strikes, takedowns, and submissions are prohibited
- Techniques must be executed with no ill intent and matches can not be won by brutality or with deliberate intent to cause injury

- Strikes must be focused and delivered in a controlled manner ensuring proper placement
- Matches are won by total score only

Section 1: Legal Striking Weapons

- Punches: reverse punch, inverted punch, and back fist
- Kicks with the instep; bottom of the foot; the blade of the foot; the ball of the foot; and toes
- Head-butting or Strikes with the head are prohibited.
- Stomping on a downed opponent and up kicks from the bottom is prohibited
- Strikes with the exception of the lower part of the foot, to the facial area, must be with the padded area of the glove or shin guard (If shin guards are being used)

Section 2: Legal Striking Targets:

- Strikes are allowed to the chest, stomach, ribs, to the face, head, kidneys, groin and/or other vital areas
- Strikes to the joints, back, spine, are prohibited
- All strikes are to be delivered to legal areas with legal striking weapons
- Strikes with malicious or deliberate intent to cause injury and excessive non-scoring strikes are prohibited

Section 3: The Following are Strictly Forbidden:

- Stalling or executing excessive non-scoring techniques
- Maliciously causing injury to an opponent
- Speaking or disrespectful conduct during the event
- Arguing with an official
- Refusing to obey the direction of any official
- Showing disregard for one's or opponent's safety
- Continuing the event outside of the competition area or

- after the referee calls for a stop
- Imposing any other condition for which the referee believes a penalty should be imposed

Section 4: Determining the Winner of the Match

- The competitor with the most recorded points at the conclusion of the match wins

Disqualification

The referee stops the event for the safety of the participant.

A final score with a two-point or fewer deficits will require a one-minute overtime period. The overtime period score will be added to the actual end of the regulation score to determine the winner of the match. One additional overtime period will be conducted if the score is an actual tie after the 1st overtime period. A sudden death period will follow if the score remains a real tie.

Scoring of Striking Techniques

Section 1: Stand-Up Striking Techniques:

- Visible contact and displacement of the body must be observed to award body striking points

2 points for:
- A kick or spinning back that clearly connects with the head of the body with proper torque, distance and follow through

1 point for:
- A punch, reverse punch, ridge hand, back fist, round-kick, side-kick, or crescent kick delivered with proper torque, distance and follow through to a legal target area of the body

No points are scored for:

- Any strike which is partially blocked to a target area
- Any strikes to the body lacking definite contact and/or displacement of the opponent's body
- Any striking technique in which the striker falls to the mat
- A clash of strikes, when there is no distinct advantage to either competitor
- Kick or Knees to legal areas of the legs

Penalties and Injuries

Section 1: Penalties

If a technique injuries a competitor, the following will determine the Referee action

- Was the technique delivered with ill intent
- Was the injury a result of no fault to either competitor
- Was the injury a result of a fighter's negligence to protect him/her
- First accidental foul/violation will result in 1 point for the fouled competitor
- Unintentional violations will result in a 1 additional point for the fouled competitor
- Third accidental violation will disqualify
- Malicious fouls may result in immediate disqualification
- Intentional strikes to illegal striking areas or with illegal striking weapons may lead to disqualification on the first offense

Section 2: Injuries

- If the event stopping injury were caused by no fault of any competitor, the victor would be determined by the score prior to an injury

- The uninjured competitor will be declared the winner in the event of a tie score with a no fault match stopping injury
- The team trainer or medical staff will have the final determination if an injured competitor may continue the event
- The injury time clock will not include consultation time of the medical personnel
- 2 minutes of injury/ recovery time is allotted to the athlete hurt by an illegal strike. The match shall be resumed at the neutral position if the injured athlete recovers and continues
- If the medical staff finds the injured athlete is unable to continue, he/she will win the match by disqualification

Section 3: Blood

- Events will immediately be halted upon the detection of blood from either competitor
- The injured competitor will have up to five minutes to stop the bleeding. The blood clock of five minutes will continue if the event is halted for additional periods of bleeding
- The maximum blood time allowed for one match is five minutes per competitor
- Once five minutes is exceeded the victor will be determined in the same manner as in Section 4: Determining the Winner of the Match.
- Each scoring table will have blood cleaning supplies for the competition area

Uniforms and Equipment

Section 1: Attire

REQUIRED AND RECOMMENDED SAFETY EQUIPMENT: the following safety equipment is required by all competitors: hand and foot pads, mouthpieces, groin cups (for male competitors only). The competitor's equipment will be checked and if it is deemed unsafe, he/she will be asked to change the equipment before he/she can compete.

- All competitors must compete with a mouthpiece
- Male competitors must wear a cup
- Female competitors may wear a chest guard
- Other protective gear such as knee pads, elbow pads, forearm guards and ear guards are optional and subject to approval by officials
- Safety equipment will be inspected prior to entering the competition area

Any taping must be approved by medical staff and/or center referee.

Hand Pads

A soft padded surface must cover the fingers, wrist and any striking surface of the hand.

Foot Pads

A soft padded surface must cover the instep, sides, toes, ankle and back of the heel of the foot. The bottom of the foot does not have to be padded.

Head Gear

The front, sides and back of the head must be covered with a soft padded surface. Equipment must be in a good state of repair and must be free of heavy taping, tears or any other repairs that may cause injury.

The tournament or event's official rules arbitrator ultimately determines the approval or denial of equipment. A properly fitted mouthpiece is required.

The competitors must compete in an approved traditional uniform for tradition divisions, forms and kata and any approved sports martial arts uniform for Kumite.

All clothing must be clean and in good repair. Buttons, zippers, metal or sharp objects are not allowed on uniforms, uniforms may have pockets as long as they are Velcro.

4 Ownership of a Master Franchise

This franchise option combines the first two choices, allows an individual or a company to own a Pro Teams KumiteSport Martial Arts Team Franchise. Operate at least one Stand-Up Against Violence Everyone (S.A.V.E) America, and also recoup franchise fees by offering Stand-Up Against Violence Everyone (S.A.V.E.) America martial arts training facilities within its defined territory. All sub-sales must be approved by the Franchisor. Pro Teams KumiteSport Martial Arts Franchise Teams will compete in all competitions organized by PTKMA locally, regionally, and nationally. A Stand-Up Against Violence Everyone (S.A.V.E.) America Franchise not only provides an opportunity to offer white belt to black belt programs and self-defense programs, but also programs that address community issues. It also offers franchisees the right to market and sell services and products of the highest standards.

Just to be clear, this franchise offering includes the added benefit of selling franchise schools within your territory. Just imagine an up and coming talentthathastheteachingskillsyou admire and respect. You as his sponsor or mentor would like to assist him or her in getting set up to teach. So, you recommend him or her for their own school franchise.Withthesupport from the corporate office and your recommendation he/she gets approved and can open a franchise school within your territory, but not within 50 miles of your school. Imagine reaping the benefits within your area of selling franchises to franchisees to recoup your franchise fees within your territory.

Here's an example of owning a territory, I was talking about California earlier. California actually has the capacity to have 3 martial arts professional teams within the state. One in the middle of California, I'd say around Los Angeles, then Southern California and, of course, northern California up around by San Francisco. So they actually have the capacity, the volume and talent to have 3 professional team franchises. Suppose somebody decides they want exclusive rights to the Los Angeles territory? Not knowing their actual numbers, i.e. the population of the city. Let's say the city population is 3 million that means that that city has the capacity to have 30 school franchises, based on 100,000 potential customer population per school. That individual would be purchasing a territory with the potential growth of 30 'S.A.V.E. Los Angeles' school franchises within that 3 million population. Split up to accommodate a minimum of 100,000 potential customer population per franchise to meet franchise requirements. The monthly fees needed to sustain a franchise within that city. So that allows the individual that purchases the team franchise. His support for his team and the participants and possible competitors would come from that area to build the franchise team. That area is where the competition would come to field the team for the Los Angeles team. The teams within the state of California would have to compete against one another eventually for an in the state-type championship before the winning team would go on to the division championship. Yes, it would cost more to have a franchise in say California that can have up to 30 sub-franchises versus say Michigan which is less densely populated? Just to make sure you have a better understanding of the franchise concept and an idea of how the franchise model would work for the Pro Teams KumiteSport Martial Arts team franchises. There would be the ownership of a Pro Teams KumiteSport Martial Arts team franchise one option; another option is the 'Stand-Up Against Violence, (S.A.V.E.) 'Name Your City' martial arts training facility which comes under the 'S.A.V.E. America' Franchise. Then there is the master franchise.

The master franchise itself includes the opportunity for territorial rights and the opportunity to sell franchises within your protected territory or assigned area to recoup your franchise fees.

So, let's go back to the league and how it would work for the franchisees. OK, let's say that you're in a state within your division and your team's been determined. You've had your annual tournament, and your team has been added to the schedule to compete in its region or division, your team events would be held at high schools within your geographic area to compete. What this is going to do is make, this type marketing of is going to allow us to brand better, get the word out about the team and league. The high schools get a chance to make money and offer up retail items for increased sales for the schools. The public will come out for entertainment. The high schools will support our PTKMA professional events by selling tickets. They'll most likely even get the high school band involved. Team events will be 2–3 hour events. The judge, referee or announcer will announce the rules so everyone can understand the rules and get a clear understanding of how the Pro Teams KumiteSport Martial Arts works and how those events will work. Over time, we'll get more and more competitors to try out for the teams. By that, increasing unit revenue through team tryouts along with more competitors becoming interested in understanding how things work and how the league works, and with that better understanding will come, more spectators.

Note: US veterans receive a 20% franchise fee discount to all new Pro Teams KumiteSport Martial Arts Franchise offerings. PTKMA supports the Veterans Transition Franchise Initiative (Vet Fran).

Requirements:

- Must perform pre-opening obligations under the Franchise Agreement
- Must have a business space of at least 3,500 square feet, preferably located near residential and business areas with accessible parking. The facility must have fire suppression sprinkler systems and accommodate 350 participants
- Must have a payment of $ 2,000.00 to $ 4,000.00 start-up package fee for Stand-Up Against Violence Everyone (S.A.V.E.) America products which form part of the initial inventory
- Must be in compliance with standards and policies

Benefits Derived from an PTKMA Franchise

Purchasing a franchise in the PTKMA, which belongs to the top 10% military franchises, provides numerous benefits and advantages to the franchisee. Easily the most visible are the existence of no other similar type of franchise in the industry and the absence of national competitors. In doing business, chances for success are far greater when the service or product being offered is unique and one-of-a-kind. PTKMA offers its franchisees access to an exclusive and proprietary product while providing support through in-depth marketing program, extensive training programs, business plan writing and on-site pre-opening assistance and an experienced support staff. The franchise business can also be established and run with minimum staffing requirements.

Other Benefits Include:

- Group marketing
- Group public relations
- Uniform/apparel sales
- School and team marketing
- Team sponsorship solicitation
- Increased tournament participation (in black belt events)
- A new circuit in which all franchisees have an equal vote for franchise decisions
- Certified judges/referees
- Added revenue from team events and black belt registrations
- Team site and link to the Pro Teams KumiteSport Martial Arts website
- Access to specialized training. All franchisees are given uniform training at the same time
- Added revenue possibilities through community-based and community-relevant programs
- Business and career opportunities for students and many more that you will get to discover when you get your PTKMA franchise

5 The League Format

My vision of a team matchup would be, at least right now, I'm thinking 3 rounds, 3 minutes, most points. The flashier the technique, the more points the one making contact with the flamboyant technique should get. The reason I suggest this strategy is because I think there's an opportunity here for being entertaining. The WWE, NBA, and the NFL are all entertaining so why not the PTKMA? As a result of movie performances of superstar martial artists like Bruce Lee, Chuck Norris and Jet Li displaying their flashy techniques. I've seen a lot of the kicks, spinning back kicks, spinning kicks to the head in the National Black Belt League, NASKA, and other tournaments across the United States and martial arts amateur circuits. In my opinion watching such flashy techniques being executed can be very exciting and quite entertaining. I think when spectators see techniques as such; you will get the 'oohs' and 'aahs'. That's what we want, excitement, flashiness, and zeal. It's like watching Michael Jordan do a 360-degree dunk.

This is nothing new; we already have competitors out there in various circuits competing that execute these techniques almost daily. This venue will give them the opportunity to showcase those talents and spectators an opportunity to enjoy them. This will give those competitors a chance to participate in their sport and entertain, within a platform the family can enjoy. I don't see a lot of families going to mixed martial arts events because of how brutal they can be. However, there is still a place for mixed martial arts.

Note: Whichever team wins the coin toss gets the added benefit of determining either the first 7 fights or the last 6 fights.

Example

The Golden Eagles out of Florida won the toss and elected to select the last 6 matches. The Ten Tigers from Atlanta chose the first 7.

Let's say we have 2 teams. Maybe one team is the Golden Eagles out of Florida the other the Ten Tigers from Atlanta. The event starts with the flipping of a coin. The team wins the toss, it lands on heads. The strategy behind the flipping of the coin allows the winner of the toss to determine the team matches for the first half of the event. He/ she determines what half of the lineup is fighting first. You have the top of the lineup to the bottom of the list, starting with the lightest weight class to the heaviest weight class. So you get the youngest aged fighters to the eldest aged fighters. Who fights first or when, would actually depend on the coin toss and would possibly change up for the second half of the event. The top half or bottom half. Depending on which team won the coin toss. The strategy could be in which fighters fight when. Knowing I have the better fighter for several weight classes could help me plan my battle strategy. It might be in my teams' best interest to have my best fighters him or her fight last so that they can make up whatever points are needed to win.

FIGHT SCHEDULE TEMPLATE				
Division	The Golden Eagles	vs.	The Ten Tigers	No.
Male 18+ Lightweight < 151	T. W.	versus	K. R.	1
Male 18+ Middleweight < 162	S. B.	versus	J. H.	2
Male 18+ Light Heavyweight <175	E. Q.	versus	S. R.	3
Male 18+ Heavyweight < 200	W. T.	versus	R. G.	4
Male 18+ Super Heavyweight > 200	B. B.	versus	J. T.	5
Male 35+ Lightweight < 162.5	J. S.	versus	J. S.	6
Male 35+ Middleweight < 173	M. M.	versus	D. W.	7
Male 35+ Heavyweight < 173	V. F.	versus	T. G.	8
Female 18+ Lightweight < 140	G. T.	versus	J. C.	9

(more next page)

FIGHT SCHEDULE TEMPLATE				
Division	**The Golden Eagles**	**vs.**	**The Ten Tigers**	**No.**
Female 18+ Lightweight > 140	R. T.	versus	J. V.	010
Female 35+ Open	S. L.	versus	R. J.	11
Coach	**M. G.**		**B. L.**	
Team manager	**T. N.**		**E. A.**	

Since the team will be fighting three 3-minute rounds, most points, at the end of the 13 matches, we will total the score. The team with the highest score at the end of the event would get a win in the 'win' column. The opposing team would get a mark as a loss in the loss column and they'd both move on to their next events. Some events may end up being the best match 2 out of 3 and they may end up coming back to that city again for another event. This, of course, depends on the schedule. Teams may fight within their division 2 to 3 times just to determine the division winner. Those decisions I don't want to make now. I would like to allow team owners an opportunity to weigh in on some decisions. I'm just trying to give readers an idea of the concept and how it could work with the teams along with how the competitions would work.

Now the reason, I picked light to medium contact for a platform with referees, is because I think that adds a little bit of drama to a sports event. In addition, that's where the majority of martial artists start. Not everybody likes referees, but most major sports, I've noticed, have rules, and there is always some issue surrounding the interpretation of what happened in an event in regards to the rules. The rules would be something that can be agreed to by the owners of the teams or they would have representation from the clubs, in the player association. I've put together a start, a rough draft of the rules as a starting point for discussion. The rules for competition are not yet etched in stone. The rules can be modified somewhat just as long as in the decision to make changes; we don't lose sight of the goal of implementing a league that caters to the majority of point competitor. The rules have been identified and laid out pretty clear. Once the league season has started, the rules will not change. Rules will be voted in or out by the players union, and implemented the following competition season.

I noticed at a lot of circuits, even though they may have judges, currently there isn't a certified judging authority. That's being worked on, but that would be something that the teams would have an opportunity to vote on, the rules. There will be a representative from each of the teams to determine the rules for the league. The guiding principle would be to develop standards and guidelines that will allow this league to grow. As we grow and build our superstars from our point competitions. We want our superstars to continue to skillfully get better and stay healthy because, injuries could prevent this. Our fan base will follow their heroes and become supporters of our league. Think about all the paraphernalia and marketing material that can come from teams that have superstars.

Through this league, we're talking about taking the amateur point martial arts superstars and turning them into professionals. Creating a league in which they can perform at a professional level because of the way we've changed the platform. For teams, registrations for the events are going to be required for the team tryouts. State eliminations events for the professional team will allow the team owners to receive revenue through registrations to pay their teams. There is value in partnering with local high schools and having events at high schools or maybe even conventions and visitors bureaus. As the league grows, some teams fan base may grow larger than others and quicker. Some teams are going to attract more spectators that other teams, and we will end up better defining those locations as we get audience support.

So the estimated startup cost for the franchises is based purely on us becoming successful. The 'S.A.V.E. America' campaign or the 'S.A.V.E. America' martial arts training facility estimated startup cost could be anywhere from $77,000.00 to $258,000.00. Of course, your cost depends on how much you already have or own of the school infrastructure, such as a building, equipment, etc. For uniformity and professionalism, we want your school to have a franchise look. Since the school franchise colors are America's colors, red, white, and blue for the S.A.V.E. your city franchise, that means S.A.V.E. franchise schools must also be red, white and blue. If you purchase a franchise school that supports a team or a franchise school with a team, then your school would then take on the colors of the team that it supports. So the more you already have or own toward the franchise or team look, the less your costs will be.

The programs or inventory of classes offered will be more like going to a college campus. If a customer comes in and they want to learn self-defense there, will be a basic self-defense and an advanced self-defense class in which they can register and attend. They will both be twelve-week classes, and that's pretty much the way they'll run things. S.A.V.E. Franchises offer courses in more like a college format. When customers come in, they register and sign up for whatever type classes they need instead of having to go through the entire white to black belt program to get whatever skills they feel they need. In addition, there will be a build your body 12-week program for those people that are overweight, trying to lose weight and get fit.

A lot of what recreation centers already do to stay competitive, martial arts studios need to consider. Even if it means modifying or making adjustments because although some martial arts schools and studios may not realize it that's their competition. Because of the issues that are presented to the community, the martial arts or S.A.V.E. your state campaign would be more effective.

Why Sport Martial Arts will Never Make the Major Leagues

First of all, some of you may ask, why do martial arts need to make the major leagues. Let's take a look at other sports, and what they offer?

What benefits do they offer?

What social benefits do they offer kids?

They help with coordination, they build self-esteem. They allow children to bond and network understand and learn sportsmanship. They also develop mental toughness teach kids how to work as a team. Let's do a side-by-side comparison. I mean when you think about major league sports, you know, there's Pop Warner leagues and middle school sports. Then there's high school, college, and the possibility of going pro.

Doing a side-by-side comparison, we can look at major league sports and martial arts since we are making a comparison between the two. I would like to add, as we make a comparison; ask yourself why it is even to this day, there is no major league for martial arts. Then, of course, there is the question, why does there need to be or is there a need for a major martial arts league, as opposed to extreme martial arts sports.

Ok, so when we look at major league sports, how are they recruited? I think the recruitment or weed out process starts as early as little league athletics when children are trying to find their athletic skills and abilities.

We can think of school athletics for all other sports except martial arts. That entry point for martial arts is the local martial arts studio, school, and/or recreation centers or instruction that offer self-defense, cardio kickboxing or another form of martial arts. We should look at this as if we are trying to build a sports dynasty or a sports league. I wonder if the other sports visionaries envisioned their games would grow into dynasties. One question would be where would the talent for my game come from? Where would the feeder schools or population come from?

As stated earlier, we know the marketing for the other major league sports start with the little league or youth leagues and then middle school, high school, and college sports. For martial arts, the marketing would come from movies and individual commercials created by the karate classes, tournaments, and, of course, really the movies.

Marketing: the schools, high school themselves they do their own marketing starting in elementary school; those Pop Warner leagues, they do their own marketing. The major league sports themselves market primarily through the help of sponsors and spectators but in doing so they also create the dream, the dream of one day being a competitor and/or participant. Of course, they do their own marketing. When you look at martial arts, there's a school, the local schools that advertise to get students. The goal, at least for most martial arts schools, is to get more students. Once they get students they, teach them. The majority of martial arts schools teach a traditional martial arts discipline. Which could be aikido, taekwondo, Shitō-ryū, Shotokan, Jeet Kune Do, Hwa Rang Do, or any one of the many hundreds of martial arts styles and disciplines that are on this earth.

Then there are the potential benefits. What are the possible benefits of major league sports? When you think of them going through those levels of school athletics: the Pop Warner sports, the middle school, high school and college, there's the possibility of college scholarships. So an individual can progress through their sport. They can take a sport, any of the major league sports, and possibly get a scholarship into a prestigious college or any college that offers their sport and have their education paid for by scholarships. Then there is, of course, the possibility of getting drafted by the pros, TV exposure, TV commercials, and then there are movies, commercials, and product endorsements.

On the martial art's side, as of this day there's the gold ring and prize money. You may be fortunate and win your division or event and win thousands of dollars and then if you're an extreme martial arts enthusiast, I think you may be getting upwards of a million dollars now. Then there are the movies and self-defense or security and protection. You know careers requiring self-defense skills like the CIA, Ranger, Special Forces and self-defense training instructors, that type of stuff.

The question was asked, why would I consider a light to medium contact venue instead of a more extreme platform as being the best platform for martial arts to be the major league venue for martial arts? To me, it's simply a numbers game. Simmons Market Research says approximately 5% of the nation at one time or another participated in the martial arts. When I travel across our great country and visit a tournament, I notice that the majority of competitors I see compete in the light-to-medium contact arena. If I were to guess, I would say 20% of martial artists compete in the extreme martial arts arena. To grow the sport, we need to have willing participants, and the more you have, the better the position you are in continuing its growth.

For the point martial arts to be considered a major league sport, I think we need to provide a 2–3 hour event in which spectators would enjoy. We as an industry haven't been successful in doing that. Another reason. In my opinion why, the light to medium contact platform would be the best platform for taking martial arts to the major leagues, is once you start growing your sport, you want to keep your superstars healthy and active to develop your sport. Point martial arts doesn't have as many injuries and your stars can participate longer, thus allowing their fans to continue supporting them.

Then there is the beauty of the American Dream as displayed in opportunities like American Idol. I think everyone at one time or another thought he or she can or could sing. People come out in large numbers to compete for those slots. You know there's only going to be so many people selected, but everybody feels that they have some musical or vocal talent or chance. So people will come out in droves to if nothing else, hear the person sing or crack up or whatever. That may not be the case when trying out for a professional sports team, but at least participants would come out in droves to secure a team position and represent their city/state. So depending on our requirements, we would make it so that everybody of a certain age would be eligible to compete. All participants would have to pay a registration fee to come out and try for the professional league. I think competitors would come out in droves. Like is done when auditioning for American Idol or the Apollo Theater in Harlem; people pay a registration fee and then they audition in hopes of getting their five minutes of fame.

Look at Tae Bo, and what it did for fitness. You know Tae Bo was actually performed in almost every martial arts studio and karate school across America. Instructors and Teachers would play music in the background and teach their students specific techniques to music, to warm up their pupils muscles before class. The instructor would warm the class up to reduce the possibility of an injury before they began getting into the actual techniques. The difference is Billy Blanks packaged the concept into a product and then sold the product nationally as Tae Bo. He took taekwondo techniques along with some boxing techniques and made them into the program we know all know as Tae Bo. He even had varying levels of difficulty.

The Extreme martial arts platform has grown very rapidly for those interested in the old Roman Coliseum events of kill or be killed. It takes a different type of mindset to get into the ring to pulverize your opponent in the extreme martial arts platform. Extreme martial arts platforms like UFC and StrikeForce are quick to be successful because it will never take them four to eight years to get a champion caliber talent. They can do it in six to eight months. Using sport martial arts, we can do the same thing. We just need a platform. For this reason, I think sport martial arts (point) will never make the major leagues because we, meaning the industry still think inside the box. We are always thinking of the tradition and allowing the martial arts to stay true to the traditional art form. I am not advocating any change. I would say at least 80% of the schools across America and possibly the world practice using safety equipment and light to medium contact to vital areas of the body. How long is a student in martial arts before he is executing the flashy kicks and techniques you might see in Bruce Lee's Enter the Dragon? Nowadays, I'd say six-to-eight months. So why don't we offer that level in our major league platform? This would keep the excitement and participation in the dojos in America and help with marketing for tournaments to get more competitors because all of them would be feeder venues for the future major leaguers training. For some reason, our industry doesn't think outside of the box. Just imagine the capabilities and what doing so can do to the growth of martial arts, and yes, I do realize this is going to upset a lot of martial arts school owners and practitioners. It already has. I have gotten very little support for making this opportunity a reality.

When I first started taking classes back in 1976, I was a beginner in the martial arts. However, I had seen numerous movies and at times would see myself trying to emulate those I had seen in the movies by an attempt to kick or punch the way they did. Within six months of taking lessons, I had my green belt and I was competing in tournaments. Before I had my green belt, I was able to kick a man in the head. I enjoyed point sparring, the exercise and the high of the competition. It was like playing tag, who can hit who first. One difference, when competing in a tournament, is you have a referee in the center of the ring. You pay your respect by bowing to the judges, bowing to him, then to each other. You understand the rules going in, no kicking below the belt, you know, no kicks to the groin depending on the type of tournament it might be. Some tournaments allow groin kicks, and cups are mandatory. At those events, there are groin kicks and other tournaments that stress no groin contact. You may not kick in the groin. Then there were those that scored more points with the flashier techniques. I have participated in tournaments where if you kick your opponent in the head you get two points. Or you connect with a spinning back kick to the head you get three points; a round kick to the head at most tournaments is one point.

I read Master Mike Stone earned his black belt in six months. So there are talented people with the capability to learn martial arts and obtain a black belt within six months. I think that's exceptional. Many individuals today, traditional martial artists, would probably say it should take at least four to six years. Depending on the style and the system and who you talk to, each system has their own level, along with their own requirements for black belt and how long it should take.

As a school owner, teacher or instructor you need to consider offering sport martial arts as a product. There, another product you can offer for sale, sport or point martial arts. That can be an entire curriculum in itself in addition to your traditional art. So if you look at it that way and you have a traditional school, this could generate more revenue for your school. In a traditional martial arts school, you may teach certain techniques and requirements for white belt. Certain procedures and requirements for a yellow belt and, of course, you may have specific requirements for green, blue, brown and so forth. Then you may have variations of the colors of the belts between those belts before they get those major belts. Traditional requirements for progression through the ranks might be what your school offers, in a nutshell. But in addition to that, let's say you have a basic self-defense course: an individual can come in off the street and learn self-defense. Not learning all of whatever is required for your white belt or your green belt or your yellow belt techniques for advancement through to black belt. Let's say a student comes to your school and they want to learn self-defense and you have a twelve-week program. Maybe you have a required amount of actual practical application hours as a requirement for completion. Say your program provides two-hour sessions and your students have to meet two times a week and the course is twelve weeks. So 48 hours of classroom instruction and practical effort is required for that certification. Then maybe you made it a certified program so each student has to take a practical exam and a written test. The actual exam, of course, is going to be their demonstration of the techniques they were taught and when they would use them. In addition, there may be a few scenarios where they have to, you know, fight their way out of or demonstrate that they are effective in what they learned. Then the written exam would be maybe a multiple guess exam; multiple choice in which the goal here is to make sure they understand, when they would use the self-defense they learned. So maybe let's say a twenty question multiple choice tests to make sure they clearly understand what was taught and when they would use their self-defense.

In addition, let's say you offer another package. A package for the individual interested in the fitness and sports aspect of martial arts, which could be the light-to-medium contact point martial arts specific to your discipline. Where they learn how to execute a side kick, the round kick, the arsenal of techniques executed from a fighting stance. You know the crescent kick, the spinning back kick, the spinning hook kick off the back leg; you know those types of techniques. The back fist, the reverse punch, the techniques one would execute from the fighting stance or the horse stance, fighting their opponent in a sport martial arts type event. The goal here would be to attract more students to your school just for the sports aspect. Not getting into the traditional perspective because maybe they can get a sport martial arts certificate, which puts them at an individual level for sport martial arts for competition. So they can compete in tournaments for the sport and exercise and the high of competition. Schools and instructors can offer programs with a certificate where they are taught the techniques required by the professional point martial arts league. You know, so maybe now they have a black belt or a brown belt in Kumite Sport light-to-medium contact. Of course, there will still be those traditional martial artists. But there will still be the extreme martial artists, UFC, strike force, and then The Pro Teams KumiteSport Martial Arts for Kumite-Sport competitors. This will allow tournament promoters another category or series of divisions of which they can add to their national competitions. The PTKMA provides a system with a built-in career progression path for martial arts artists, trainers and teachers. Schools can train on what's needed and a league can emerge. At present, we can't honestly compare to other major league sports because we have never provided a comparable platform. I think that's important to understand.

Let's look closely at baseball. With baseball, I think a pre-school age child can start off playing T-ball. They have a little stick out of the ground with a ball on it, and they swing the bat to get their swinging technique. Then as they get older, they can play little league baseball and then from there is high school ball and then of course college ball. But these progressions allow these kids to take advantage of the benefits that I spoke of earlier. With baseball, let's think about it, you have a referee or you have an umpire who calls the signals behind the plate; a person pitches the ball and they swing and they hit the ball. The ball goes over the fence that's a home run. Get three people on base and somebody hits a home run with three people on the base and you have a grand slam, 4 points. A person hits the ball ends up on first base he has the single; he gets a double, triple, etc., etc. At the end of nine innings, the team with the most points wins the game. They get a win in the win column the loser gets a one in the loss column. So that's pretty much baseball and how scoring works. The game continues as long as it takes to play nine innings, each of which is over when each team gets three outs per inning. You have nine people on the field for one team and nine for the other.

In single competition sports like martial arts or wrestling it's up to the skill of each individual. With the team strategy, I'm proposing with coaches, and the team roster order of competition will add more of a challenge for teams to win. If one team member is not up to snuff the whole team will not suffer because the other team scores a lot of points on that weakest player. This will put more stress on every player and not weed out the "weak" martial artists.

In baseball, you have a pitcher, a catcher, so they have positions. First base, second base, shortstop, third base, center field, outfield, left field, right field and of course center field. So those are the team positions for baseball when I talk about baseball that's pretty standard for all baseball leagues. There is consistency from school to school because it's a well-established set of rules for baseball that whatever school you go to they follow those rules. They follow those rules. So children grow understanding the fundamentals and standards and how to play the sport. I would say those are feeder schools or farm teams. A training ground that creates an opportunity for kids to understand, really learn fielding, grounding, baseball, batting, hitting, throwing, all the fundamentals and concepts so they can elevate to the other levels. You know high school, college and possibly pro.

Next let's talk about football. Football is not that different. In football, the players are also on a team. There are eleven players on the field at any given time. You have offense and defense. They use a ball which they call a football which is oblong oval shaped and the game is broken down into quarters. The team has captains. They meet at the beginning of the competition. They flip a coin and from there they make a decision on which team is going to receive the ball and be offense, try to score first, and which team is going to return the kick-off. The receiving team is the offense and the team kicking is defense. At any given time, the team with the ball is on offense. Their goal is to pass or run the ball from their side of the field into the other team's end zone and get a touchdown. When they get a touchdown, they score six points and then there's the extra point which is kicked. It is called a field goal. There is a kicker who kicks the ball through the goalposts to receive the seventh point, and that is how they get their points. The game is divided into quarters, which can be anywhere from twelve to fifteen minutes, depending on whether it is college or professional. Kids end up playing as early as age 6–8 years old in Pop Warner football depending on location or early development. Due to the NFL, the sport of football has gotten so huge they have recreation centers that organize leagues to play. Even flag football, where the runner's flag is pulled instead of tackling. The marketing for football is so enormous and tremendous it is not hard to get people interested in playing football. I would say the super bowl has added a great deal of visibility for fans and excitement. From the super bowl year to year and the individual teams that play. There are thirty-two teams in the NFL, and they are broken down by divisions. There can be as many as eight teams in each division and then those groups are split again. The teams that compete against each other, they have half backs and quarterbacks that are team positions. One rule in football is only certain people can run the ball like the ends, tight ends and running backs, fullbacks, and the quarterback. Defensive players are on the opposing team, and their goal is to stop or prevent the other team from scoring.

So football has positions and martial arts have individual practitioners, along with weight classes? The power of football and other team sports is that you have the camaraderie of working together. No matter how good your quarterback is you can't win with a star quarterback alone—you need good blockers and running backs and wide receivers and the team working together as a team to win. In martial arts, it seems you also need good people, but it's much clearer who the better team members are because they get the most points. This makes the people, who get fewer points, feel like they are less skilled than the star of the team and can demoralize those people. Like baseball, once again the team with the most points from scoring touchdowns or field goals wins. Any time a kicker or team gets within field goal range within the NFL. I guess that's within fifty or fifty-five yards from the goal. I think the record is 62 yards, a person kicks a field goal and if it goes through the uprights of the goal, then they score three points. The teams continue to play until time runs out. The team with the most points at the end of the game wins the game. The best teams from each of the divisions compete against one another to determine who's going to compete in the super bowl, which is football's national championship. A football game usually lasts four full quarters, or like I said earlier, each being either twelve to fifteen minutes or maybe even as little as six minutes for the Pop Warner leagues. But the goal is everybody, school, elementary, they understand the four quarter concept, they know the players and they grow up learning the fundamentals of the sport.

Basketball is also somewhat similar. However, they use a round ball that is bounced or as they call it, you dribble the ball; there are only five players on the court at any given time. Oh yeah, they play on a basketball court, indoors. In basketball, they have fouls, which are like penalties. Football draws a penalty whenever somebody does something that's against the rules. Then they may be penalized. When there is a foul the person ends up, the person that executes the foul on the player, they get a foul marked against them. Once they get six fouls they, are ejected out of the game. The player that they offend or foul gets an opportunity to shoot for extra points. A free throw depending on where they are on the court, to get points. Every time there's a basket made, somebody shoots the ball and it goes into the basket they get two points. If they're at a certain range beyond the foul line, they can score as many as three points if they make the shot.

They also play four quarters. Their quarters can also be anywhere from twelve to fifteen minutes depending on whether it's high school or college basketball, and then the team with the most points wins. They get a one in the win column. The other team gets a one in the loss column.

Hockey: I'm not that familiar with the game, as I didn't play hockey. However, I do know they have a puck they play with. The sport is played on ice, with hockey sticks, masks, and equipment. Play starts in the center of the rink. They also have team positions. You have an opposing team and you have the other teams. During an event, you have two teams competing against one another and there is a goal. Any time the puck is struck from one side to the other end of the goal, nonstop by the goalie then it's a point. At the end of the game, of course, they also play periods. Their game is divided into periods like the other sports. Once again, they get participants accustomed to playing by an industry-established set of rules. To add to the entertainment, some sports have halftime shows: half time events allow the coaches that last opportunity to talk strategy with the team players and possibly change the outcome of the game.

So, what makes martial arts different? Firstly, martial art is viewed as an extreme sport. I think from what I've seen, the techniques demonstrated or displayed at these events, the hands wrapped, taped and stuffed into boxing gloves, depending on which venue or platform you've seen. I remember watching the Professional Karate Association (PKA). I was fortunate in having the pleasure of training and working out with Richard Jackson as he was preparing for his first professional full contact karate match. He would train 3 rounds of boxing and then three rounds of sparring but because of the power of his spinning back fist he would come to rely on that technique. In boxing, the knockout or the executor of it is King, or whoever can deliver the knockout first, is the King. Throughout his training, I noticed that he had to wear boxing gloves; he ended up focusing more on his boxing techniques. One rule of the Professional Karate Association (PKA) was each competitor had to perform six kicks per round as a minimum. So once you executed your six kicks. Then you could box during the rest of the round. A lot of boxers migrated over from boxing. Boxers that weren't doing that well as professional boxers saw an opportunity in the PKA and transitioned to kickboxing in the PKA. A lot of them might box one-week end in a boxing match and the next weekend participate in a PKA event. I noticed again, in the World Combat League (WCL), Chuck Norris introduced his team concept. Which I think was excellent but in my opinion it failed because he didn't take into consideration what they learned from the PKA and make the changes needed for the WCL to be successful. The PKA actually lasted longer than the WCL.

I personally attempted the first team league back in 2002. I presented my team concept at Dewey Earwood's tournament in Columbia, South Carolina at the Sheraton Hotel to a host of martial artists that follow point competition. I was then employed by Bank of America. I was trying to understand why there hadn't been any changes made to point martial arts events. I was at least expecting them to offer more compensation for martial artists ready to graduate from amateur point competition. I actually left martial arts for a time, from 1986 to 1997. As I stated earlier, I returned to competition back in 1997 and noticed there had been no change. I was surprised to learn that after 70 plus years of martial arts in America there has been no real noticeable change to the point martial arts industry. There are hundreds of martial arts tournament circuits that are still operating as separate entities with no uniformity whatever. For some reason, we just can't get along, despite Ed Parker hosting this huge tournament in Los Angeles and martial arts having been in America way before then. I remember seeing a movie, I want to say it was or included Sterling Silliphant, or back in the day it was a movie that included a judo expert. To this day, I would remember this film if I saw it again. Judo has been practiced in America well over seventy, eighty years, and judo, of course, is in the Olympics. It has an established set of rules for competition. Anybody that wants to compete at that level must learn and follow those rules.

What I'm proposing, is, first of all, let's understand what makes martial arts the sport different. Is it the people? Is it the perception? Is it what we, the industry, think people think the major leagues for the martial art should be? Is it how effective your style or art should be?

When we offer something in martial arts and we present it to the public, does it have to end with a knockout? Does it have to be demonstrated to the public as being more devastating than boxing? Or should that be the dark part of the art? Do we always have to use boxing techniques, as if the martial arts techniques aren't sufficient enough? Are there not enough practical techniques in martial arts to use?

So I want to be the first to go on record and say that maybe it's the rules, the rules that are chosen. All of our major TV platformed events seem to adopt or use boxing's jab and, of course, the knockout. Why are we so compelled to compete with boxing using boxing techniques? Martial Arts have a hefty inventory of lethal techniques. Maybe demonstrations of how deadly a martial artist can be in his own element might be critical.

If we have to go where the money is, we all know successful boxers can get paid in the millions of dollars when they are at the prize fighting level like "Money" Floyd Mayweather. I don't think other than Ultimate Fighting Championships (UFC) will you find martial artist getting paid that level of income; maybe in the extreme sport such as ultimate fighter type championships like Strike Force.

So I have to say that the rules and the game itself may be a factor in getting us that major platform. There is also the fact that people expect it to be so brutally violent and efficient, with the gloved hands we should be able to knock somebody out. For our industry marketing has been primarily movies, tournaments, and local martial arts schools. More realistically marketing for martial arts, has been venues such as the World Combat League (WCL), the Professional Karate Association (PKA), ISKA. So when parents see these events, I think in their minds they envision their children in that type of environment when attending a martial arts school. Could this image possibly be hurting martial arts school enrollment? All of the martial arts events I've seen when it comes to offering a professional level event; there is this need to continually market the knockout. Well, martial arts industry, there is a new sheriff in town and his signature move is the rear-naked choke. What else can we pull out of our arsenal? We do have an array of flashy techniques, how about the jump spinning back kick to the stomach? How long do you think it will take to master that technique? I would like to be the first to say that I believe it is in the best interest of martial arts and its growth that we market and promote (point) sport martial arts in America. Also, take the light to medium (point) sport martial arts platform and present it to America as a professional sport. This in my opinion would be best for marketing martial arts. The more extreme martial art can still be yet another product offered by schools for those that are interested. How do I plan to market point martial arts you might ask? First of all, think two-hour platform or a two to three-hour event. That's the way we need to package our event at first. All other major league sports have a two-three hour product for entertainment. But the other thing, to consider, is that kids four and five years old are already starting to learn martial arts. Also, remember we have a bullying problem and self-defense needs throughout America. This problem won't go away overnight. A football player can be bullied, so can a martial artist, but if he is taught how to defend his or herself and understands how to protect and how to apply what he or she has learned. I think there is value in them learning so. Martial arts has value, self-discipline, and confidence, courage and coordination which are something that team sports like baseball, football, basketball and hockey all require along with self-discipline. The majority of team sports also require a person to put their ego aside and work as a team. Ball hogs in basketball only end up earning the enmity of their team-mates. A quarterback needs to coordinate with his running backs and wide receivers while trusting in the defensive line. A pitcher needs to coordinate with his catcher to strike batters out and relies on his basemen and outfielders to stem the tide of runners if the other team hits the ball. The Total Martial Arts Concept opens the door to expanded opportunities beyond the current martial arts landscape.

If martial arts became a national sport, and part of an effective sports program across America, such as little league baseball, football and/or hockey as not all of these sports are embraced throughout America. I think this would help grow martial arts and enhance the opportunity to graduate our amateur point martial artist and build a professional sport. I think that's the best chance for martial arts. Should we consider providing a major league platform for martial arts? I think so. I've explained the best possible program in detail in this book. So how would that look? Maybe there's a team, or should I say thirty-two teams; perhaps we mirror the NFL with thirty-two teams. I have taken a stab in selecting thirty-two cities across America. Thirty-two states with the most martial arts schools. My position is those states have the most participation, but that can be proven wrong by the number of requests I get through the PTKMA website. In my opinion, the best model is to have thirty-two large tournaments across America that determines the teams for the Pro Teams KumiteSport Martial Arts. Within those states are the cities, where these events will be held. Each year having team tryouts to determine the best to represent the city/state over time, will allow the league to grow and build. In addition, it will create an opportunity for the owners, the tournament promoters, to reap financial rewards from a source other than their tournaments after the eliminations have been held. These competitions will take place annually. Each team would have a coach and a team manager selected for that team to represent its city. The group would serve the city/state in the league and the owner will reap the financial benefits as is done by other franchise team owners. Consider looking at it from the top down: growing the martial arts to a major league and for point martial arts to be a major league sport. It has to be available to the masses. The sport has to be mastered in a short period of time, 8–12 months to keep the schools full and the training grounds packed. It has to be accessible to all. It has to be a sport where the majority of competitors can seize the opportunity to compete and secure those team positions. If we used a city like Los Angeles, California as an example, in California alone there are over two thousand martial arts schools. There are forty thousand martial art studios in the United States. In Los Angeles, dividing the state up into thirds, the upper, lower and middle, maybe there are six hundred schools supporting each team. From those six hundred schools, we can determine the best thirteen martial artists, a manager, and a coach to represent Los Angeles. Also, that team will compete against the other teams within its division for an annual championship like the Super Bowl, The Pennant or any other sports national championships. Since the pool of talent in each state isn't equal, the probability that locations with the highest population density, such as LA and New York City, may have the greater talent. Say you have a pool of 2000 martial arts schools in California that might be 20,000 martial artists, maybe less. Compare 2000 martial arts schools to say 200 in south-eastern Michigan. The law of probability would suggest that LA would churn out more talented people than Michigan would. You would have states or teams that would become known to be the "champion" states that are unbeatable while the states with lower populations by proportion would be last. Through the Total Martial Arts Concept, there would be regional and division championships. This competition would only make martial arts better. Over time championship team competitors and/ or coaches would eventually retire or relocate and/or management and coaching talent would get hired locally or transfer to needed areas and eventually become coaches. Once the concept catches on, relocation would be a possibility for managers. Managers will seek out opportunities and competitors will chase titles, fame, and money. For this reason spreading their wealth of knowledge to other states, for this reason, enhancing martial arts throughout the nation, which is all good for martial arts.

Both professional and college leagues do not pull from the population of their region for talent but instead pull from around the country. Professional players in the NFL and other sports are recruited from colleges around the nation and those colleges recruit players from high schools around the country, relatively making college and professional leagues even. The talented players go to these locations where these prestigious teams are, rather than the colleges just drawing from whoever is within a 50-mile radius. Franchise school owners will offer scholarships for martial arts, some schools are doing this today but with a professional point league, this might bring more value. PTKMA competitors are not going to move to a different region to participate in a point martial arts league if there isn't a financial incentive greater than the social and monetary cost of moving to that area. With this mind, it is understood that league competitors may have to start with small salaries such as done in semi-pro football where players are paid $200 a game. We realize without fat salaries or big pay days. Initially, we may not be able to attract top talent until the concept catches on and the popularity grows. Within the first two years, competitors should be able to get paid as much as $500 per event. That is not bad for 9 minutes of work. With increased opportunity comes increased compensation for promoters and competitors. So let's put this in perspective. With the Total Martial Arts

Concept, it's not just an individual going to a tournament chasing points. He or she now can be chasing points all the way up to his brown belt, while getting fighting experience to the next level, Pro Sport: The Pro Teams KumiteSport Martial Arts. Let's say we open up competition so brown belts and black belts can compete on the same platform. After all, we are only talking light to medium contact. Winning competitors can represent their city or state in a national championship. Then each year this city/state tournament will determine the best of the best with the division winners being the team to represent that city or state in the national championship. In doing so, I think we've expanded the possibilities exponentially. This may only excite promoters.

Now I present to you why I think there will never be, why I believe that martial arts will never make the major leagues. I think it is because we are so spread out; we as an industry are so diverse, dis-enfranchised, with our own ways of thinking. We lack the unity needed to implement a major league sport. There are over five hundred amateur circuits across America, 500. That's a lot. There are over forty thousand schools in the United States. There is a circuit growing every day. One person or a set of people or a group of individuals get upset because of what one person says or the way one person did something at a tournament or whatever. Like immature children, they take their toys and find another sandbox in which to play: one in which they can create their own rules to follow. Major league sports do not allow that immaturity. Then they take their tournament, leave and start up their own circuit. However, that is good because I think all these circuits and schools can be feeder tournaments and schools for a professional point league. Competitors will still need to hone skills; they will need continued practice, to elevate the level of competition. Competitors will need to keep honing their skills to stay in shape. Tournaments will be the vehicle to get them to that level. A standard of this caliber should allow martial arts competitions to grow in numbers across America and other countries. Providing a professional platform for point martial artists, thus enabling them to graduate from the amateur level point competition and giving them the opportunity to compete at a higher standard, and getting paid to do so. Making that competition available to the masses in their city-state to determine the best of the best to represent the state. I think that is only going to promote and market martial arts like the NFL does for football.

My Team Owner Recommendations

The following list of possible candidates is of people I've either come to know or have attended one of their annual tournaments. These individuals are focused and truly understand what it takes to have an A-rated tournament.

I made the list to show you that there definitely are individuals and groups whom I believe would be willing to work with you in the location that you are interested in.

These are individuals that already have successful annual tournaments. It wouldn't take much from them in making their annual competition the actual team tryout event for their states professional martial arts team.

Because this is a publication, I cannot disclose the names and organizations listed. I would encourage you to call me to discuss possibilities. I will be able to tell you the individuals I listed here.

Best-Known Candidates for Team Ownership

The Northeastern Division		
Team Name		**Team Owner - Prospect**
The Woukou Pirates	Detroit, MI	R. P.
The Shaolin Warriors	Newburgh, NY	B. L.
The Five Animals	Chelsea, MA	N. S.
The Black Emperor	New Haven, CT	H. B.
The Red Lotus	Chester, PA	B. V.
Ten Tigers	Cleveland, OH	R. L.
The Midnight Assassins	Atlantic City, NJ	I. M.
The Golden Eagles	Indiana	D. M.

The Southeast Division		
Team Name		**Team Owner - Prospect**
Snake Fist Fighters	Kentucky	R. S.
The Street Fighters	Memphis, TN	C. R.
The Dragon	Virginia	R. F.
Shaolin White Snake	Baltimore, MD	J. B.
The Mantid	South Carolina	D. E.
108 Locking Hands	Rocky Mount, NC	E. D.
The Five Elders	Homestead, FL	M. M.
The Eight Immortals	Atlanta, GA	G. R.

The Pacific Division		
Team Name		**Team Owner - Prospect**
Knights of Darkness	Washington	J. A.
Forest Ghosts	Oregon	D. W.
The Death Squad	California	S. C.
The 36th Chamber	Nevada	J. F.
Masters of the Eight Laws	Utah	B. L.
The Iron Monkey	Arizona	S. K.
Thirty-Six Families	New Mexico	L. H.
Komodo	Colorado	D. C.

The Midwestern Division		
Team Name		**Team Owner - Prospect**
The Venom Squad	Weslaco, TX	T. L.
The Redfist Clan	Muskogee, OK	D. F.
The White Crane	Kansas	S. P.
The Black Cobra	Alexandria, LA	C. B.
The Golden Centipede	St. Louis, MO	B. L.
The Poison Clan	East St. Louis, IL	L. T.
The 9 Dragons	Milwaukee, WI	J. C.
7 Clans of Kung Fu	Minneapolis, MN	L. C.

6 Getting Sponsors

The popularity of martial arts may be nowhere near that of football here in the United States. That does not mean this is entirely due to lack of interest. In fact, Simmons Market Research recently reported that over 18.1 Million Americans participated in some form of martial arts during the year 2013. This only goes to show, that the languishing martial arts scene in this country is not due to the lack of potential participants, but because of the lack of organization. There have been no previous attempts to seriously professionalize point martial arts.

We are the only organization wholly committed to professionalizing point martial arts. This includes the light to medium contact martial arts styles that utilize safety equipment (hands, feet, and headgear) and award points for making contact to vital areas. These martial arts styles include but not limited to taekwondo and many other disciplines. However, all martial arts disciplines are familiar with the term Kumite. We are the lone rangers on this concept of professionalizin' where the many of martial artist practice, sport (point) martial arts. The Pro Teams KumiteSport Martial Arts Franchise, LLC has taken the first step in professionalizing the amateur martial arts tournament level competition into a major league sport with the first ever Pro Teams KumiteSport Martial Arts.

Sponsor Benefits

The Pro Teams KumiteSport Martial Arts is presenting an opportunity to partner as a Sponsor or Vendor of the first league where the best of the best light-to-medium point sports martial artist compete for a national championship. Martial artists will secure team positions and represent their city/state in the national championship of thirty-two teams like is done in all the main league sports. Your company will receive valuable recognition across a highly sought after demographic. With a comprehensive benefits package, your business will significantly benefit from an association with the PTKMA.

The following outlines the benefits you will get as a sponsor of the Pro Teams KumiteSport Martial Arts:

Title Sponsor

- Your company will be the official sponsor of the Pro Teams KumiteSport Martial Arts with naming rights—3-year agreement

- Verbal acknowledgment and thank you at league events

- Company name and logo on official event bags and all event t-shirts of participants, judges, scorekeepers and staff

- Exhibit space booth with approved signage—consists of a 6-ft table

- Acknowledgment and link on PTKMA website: (www. thenationalmartialartsleague.com). Company name/logo to be included in event material used for television, newspapers, magazines, the internet, radio, posters and other mediums used for the advertising of league events. Effective from the date of sponsorship

- Signage as venue configuration allows

- Five minutes to directly address the attendees, and present awards at annual awards banquet

- Meet and greet with photo and marketing opportunities with winning teams. Signed glossy of winning team(s)

- Name and logo on awards as title sponsor

- Name and logo recognition on awards presentation table and printed program at annual awards banquet
- Twenty-five (25) exhibitor seasons passes for league events
- 250-word company description for program booklets
- Press release opportunity
- Access to Most Valuable Competitor (MVC) for potential marketing opportunities
- A one-time use of the listing of all participants of the PTKMA
- Coupons and/or advertisements for attendee packets
- Opportunity to present at annual awards banquet
- Hotel accommodations and table for four (4) at the annual awards banquet

Team Sponsor

32 Teams, one sponsor for each

- Verbal acknowledgment and thank you in each team event.
- Recognition and link on PTKMA website. Company name/logo to be included in PTKMA event paraphernalia, and materials used for television, newspaper, magazines, the internet, radio, posters and other mediums used during the advertising of the sports event. Effective from date of sponsorship
- Signage as venue configuration allows
- Two minutes to directly address attendees and present as team sponsor at group events
- Meet and greet with photo and marketing opportunities with winning team participants at the qualifying tournament. Signed glossy of winning (competitors) that make up the team
- Name and logo recognition on awards presentation table, printed program at annual awards banquet
- Your company logo on official team bag
- Ten (10) exhibitor seasons passes for league events
- 100-word company description for program booklet

- Press release opportunity
- Access to Most Valuable Team Competitor (MVC) for potential marketing opportunities
- Team uniform color selection and naming rights to be presented by sponsor at awards ceremony
- Logo on sponsored team uniform for the league season, Logo on the team bus as a team sponsor for League season (per PTKMA requirements)
- A one-time use of the listing of all participants of the PTKMA team-sponsored
- Coupons and/or advertisements for league event attendee packets
- Attendance for two (2) at the annual awards banquet

Diamond Sponsor

- Verbal acknowledgment and thank you at each PTKMA event.
- The opportunity to exhibit space/sponsor (vendor) booth with approved signage—consists of a 6-ft table at all PTKMA league events
- Business card drawing for the prize
- Two minutes to directly address the attendees during league season event midpoints
- Eight (8) exhibitor passes to league events
- 75-word company description for program booklets
- Coupons and/or advertisements for attendee packets

Platinum Sponsor

- Verbal acknowledgment and thank you at each PTKMA event
- The opportunity to exhibit space/sponsor (vendor) booth with approved signage—consists of a 6-ft table at all PTKMA league events
- Business card drawing for the prize

- Two minutes to directly address the attendees during league season event midpoints
- Five (5) exhibitor passes to league events
- 50-word company description for program booklets
- Coupons and/or advertisements for attendee packets

Gold Sponsor

- Verbal acknowledgment and thank you at each PTKMA event
- The opportunity to exhibit space/sponsor (vendor) booth with approved signage—consists of a 6-ft table at all PTKMA league events
- Business card drawing for the prize
- Two minutes to directly address the attendees during league season event midpoints
- Three (3) exhibitor passes to league events
- 25-word company description for program booklets
- Coupons and/or advertisements for attendee packets

Annual Awards Banquet Sponsor

- Two-minute verbal acknowledgment and thank you at the event
- Exhibit space/sponsor (vendor) booth with approved signage—consists of a 6 ft. Table
- Business card drawing for the prize.
- Coupons and/or advertisements for attendee packets
- Distribution of product at the event
- Sampling opportunities
- Category exclusivity

Annual Awards Refreshment Break Sponsor

- One-minute verbal acknowledgment and thank you at the event
- Exhibit space/sponsor (vendor) booth with approved signage—consists of a 6-ft table
- Business card drawing for the prize
- Coupons and/or advertisements for attendee packets
- Distribution of product at the event
- Sampling opportunities
- Category exclusivity

Annual Event Product Sponsor(s)

Unlimited

- One-minute verbal acknowledgment and thank you at event sponsored
- Exhibit space/sponsor (vendor) booth with approved signage—consists of a 6-ft table
- Business card drawing for the prize
- Coupons and/or advertisements for attendee packets
- Distribution of product at league events
- Sampling opportunities
- Category exclusivity

Vendor Booths per Event—Choice

- Exhibit space/sponsor (vendor) booth with approved signage—consists of a 6-ft table
- Business card drawing for the prize
- Coupons and/or advertisements for attendee packets
- Distribution of product at the event
- Sampling opportunities

Current Sponsors

TBA

Advertisement in Event Brochure

Your company will receive promotional support and presence throughout the PTKMA League Season. Specifically, your business will be entitled to the following:

Make an impact on the attendees the moment they enter an PTKMA Event. Even after they are back home by placing an ad in the widely used and highly visible PTKMA League Events Program Booklet to be distributed at 16 events per week during the competition season. This book will be circulated to all attendees, competitors, judges, staff, exhibitors, etc. Ad space is available in full, half, quarter and business card sizes.

- Back cover (color) (Exclusive)
- Full-page ad
- Half-page ad
- Quarter-page ad
- Business card ad

As a sponsor or vendor of the PTKMA team eliminations, your company will receive valuable recognition across a highly sought after demographic. With a comprehensive benefits package, your business will significantly benefit from an association with the historic event. The following outlines the term associated with the opportunity:

Pro Teams KumiteSport Martial Arts sponsorship opportunity

Term

3 years

Contact Information

Mailing address:

>Dexter V. Kennedy, President
>The Pro Teams KumiteSport Martial Arts, LLC
>208 Majestic Drive
>Columbia, SC 29223

Email address:

>dexterkennedy@hotmail.com

Cell phone: (803) 665-8453

Note: Please go to "Connect with Dexter Kennedy" on page 171 for more contact information.

7 What I've Learned

What have I learned? This has been a very educational 19 years. I made an attempt to create a professional point martial arts league in 2003. I hired 10 people, we traveled to various cities: West Chester, Pennsylvania, Biloxi Mississippi, Atlanta, Georgia, Towson, Maryland and some other cities. We had 11 sponsors, 11 cities—and no one showed up. Our website, thekumite.com, showed a tremendous amount of activity. We posted the events online and no one showed up. We had numerous calls from different cities inquiring about the event. I actually sent people from my company to each of the 11 cities and we may have had one to two to three participants actually show up.

I have an idea that has not been tested or proven. I came up with this idea, simply from being a competitor. I had gone to a number of events and a number of tournaments and noticed that the champions of tournaments had nowhere else to go, once they had won consistently and won hundreds of tournaments. There was nowhere else no higher level of competition. So I figured I would take on this opportunity this challenge. I withdrew a large sum of money from my retirement account to franchise this concept I call, the Pro Teams KumiteSport Martial Arts.

When I purchased the website thenationalmartialartsleague.com, the website designer, the developer, pretty much just put up the site. He apparently wasn't that knowledgeable in SEO and neither was I. In 2002, I personally set up the first website thekumite.com. My company and I were led to believe we had a lot of activity on our website. Our new website, thenationalmartialartsleague.com, wasn't set up with SEO either.

I hosted an event in Columbia, South Carolina. The goal was to sign 32 teams to contract and have them perform as teams within the Pro

Teams KumiteSport Martial Arts. It wasn't wise of me to think that in South Carolina, with a Confederate flag displayed daily on the statehouse grounds. For some reason, I didn't believe that would matter. Another bad idea, I thought through advertising and marketing I could get people to come from the other 49 states to Columbia. I figured that If I got them to register they would come and compete to secure positions for the 32 teams needed to compete in my professional point league of martial arts, the Pro Teams KumiteSport Martial Arts. I didn't clearly understand the market. There are 40,000 plus schools across the United States, here in America. There are over 500-point martial arts amateur circuits, including the American Taekwondo Association.

It was assumed that school owners would be perfect buyers for these teams, owners of these professional martial arts teams in the national league. I learned that most school owners are living student to student. Or paycheck to paycheck and cannot afford to purchase and own a professional team for their state. At least from the ones I had spoken with as of this writing. Most owners are entirely focused on the day-to-day activities and operations of their schools and students. Thinking of what's going on in the local community and the programs they have within their local schools. I let advertisers convince me that those individuals coming out of the military would be interested in my franchise concept and purchase. I also bought advertising with military-friendly franchising. We received over 50 leads, had a link to their website. Interested parties can complete an online form and their information is sent directly to our company email, allowing us to collect their address and number and send them a franchise brochure and packet. Fifty leads, no sales. I personally spoke with a large number of those leads by phone. We were getting quite a bit of leads; so, we decided to send franchise brochures. The brochure is about 9 pages. It included a franchise brochure, application and the franchise benefits of ownership along and a letter asking them to call us, should they have any questions or need additional information. We offered 50 percent discounts on franchise fees and start-up costs, still, no sales. I listened to the company that helped me franchise my idea and they pretty much told me that I needed to consider a martial arts school franchise in my offering. Because, initially, I went to the franchise company, to franchise the concept for a professional team league for martial arts like in the NFL, and not for a martial arts school. One may wonder why we didn't consider large restaurant franchises, and research how they got started, like McDonalds, for example, beginning with a few company-owned restaurants and once they were established then start franchising. Which I think is an excellent idea? The issue is time. The quickest route to success in this venture is to partner with those that have already been successful. There will be those that fully understand the benefits and concept and will gladly jump on the bandwagon. Of course, there will be some negotiation. Some promoters are more established than others and bring a lot more to the table.

After a review of all of our franchise documents, it made perfect sense to me that we include a franchise for a martial arts school. The martial arts school franchise is for those individuals interested in owning a school, but may be challenged finding the funding, the financial support needed to get their project off the ground. Think of yourself as an instructor or a school owner, and you have a prime candidate from your school that you would like to recommend for ownership of a school. One of your students with a great deal of potential and promise. One you feel confident with expanding your craft, the art along with the knowledge and your teachings. Wouldn't you like to help him/her own a school or teach in a school? So you've finally decided you want to help the individual and then you are faced with obstacles or issues in the person getting the funding and financing they need to get started. These were considered when I defined the Pro Teams KumiteSport Martial Arts Franchise concept.

We realize that every person isn't capable of successfully running a business. Just because someone is skilled in martial arts does not mean they would make a good franchisee. For this reason, we think it would be best to reach out to entrepreneurs (existing school owners). Have them expand, modify or convert their existing school to fit our franchise model then trust in talented martial artists who may have a passion, but no business sense and run the franchise brand into the ground. The only thing worse than having no franchisees is to have franchisees that, through mismanagement, cause a franchise to fail in the early days, reflecting poorly on the organization that backed them. We feel strongly about reaching out to those that currently own successful martial arts businesses. Those that know what's required to be successful will only recommend those that meet the requirements needed to run a successful martial arts business.

Also, the school itself was called the Kumite Fight Club. I think the name Kumite Fight Club didn't add any value and, in fact, made the franchise less marketable. We have since changed the name to S.A.V.E. America: Stand Up Against Violence Everyone (S.A.V.E.) or S.A.V.E. plug in your city state. So this means the school franchise name would be something like "S.A.V.E. Detroit." This is the new franchise name. The goal of this franchise is to provide assistance to the franchisee in assessing his/her area of the city for the best classes for success. We do this by having a team evaluate the community, determine the top 10 issues of the community and then the school itself will provide value within that community by offering programs to combat the issues identified. Typical community issues across America have been bullying and the need for a 12-week self-defense fundamental and advanced program. Instead of going to a martial arts school and having to go to class every day. For two to five years to get a black belt, before you truly feel confident and know how to defend yourself. The S.A.V.E. America Franchise would almost be like attending college; allowing you to pick the classes that you need, say maybe a self-defense course. After you've completed the self-defense course and received your certificate. You decide whether you want to continue and go for a black belt. Then you can register and take the classes needed to complete from beginner all-the-way through black belt.

I lost thousands of dollars setting up at trade shows. What a waste. The first trade show, I was scheduled to participate in, was in DC. DC requires that you be a registered franchise company within the district to attend or you will have to pay hefty fines. The process for registration was quite timely. I wasn't given enough time prior to the trade show event to register with the district. The fees for registration were $300-$500, and the cost of the trade show was another $2495. The company that scheduled the trade show didn't care whether you were legally registered and didn't do any due diligence or offer any type of a refund. You are required as a franchise to do your own due diligence and your own research before you pay them to participate. Not knowing or being informed to do so could cost you thousands in fines. You could be wasting your money and still have to pay hefty fees, fines and penalties and never be the wiser until the day of the show. The only kind of assistance the franchise trade show company would offer was credit towards the next franchise show. Fifty percent off, which means we would have to pay again twice to cover our initial cost but that would mean we paid double. Their comment was, "Well, we already paid for your booth. Even though you didn't show up, we are going to have to pay for your booth." So that was a bust. The next one was in Atlanta.

The PTKMA at Trade Show Atlanta 2014

Our booth at the Trade Show in Atlanta

We set up a table in Atlanta. Although, we only had to pay half of the booth fee, they gave us 50% credit from the prior mishap so we ended up paying $1250—so we set up a table. We collected 100 leads that weekend. We were told all leads were pre-qualified. We followed up. We even had a drawing. We had a great turnout, passed out hundreds of business cards. We followed up on our leads, responded back to them, no sales. We weren't able to turn those into any successful franchise sales.

I spent a great deal of money in press releases and a lot of time and money in writing press releases. I probably have over 500 press releases on the Internet. There's definitely a great deal of information about the Pro Teams KumiteSport Martial Arts on the internet. Those press releases are apparently allowing people to find us; when they find us, they know what we're doing. Through the press releases, we haven't received any valid leads or any news opportunities for that matter. Sidney called from the Terry Bradshaw show. The Terry Bradshaw show wanted $60,000 for us to be on their show. We also received a call from a newsman-like Mike Wallace; I can't think of his name right now—but it was going to cost us yet another $30,000 to be on his show.

New Shows Studios found us and called us, as a result of the press releases. It was going to cost us anywhere from $5000-$10,000. $5000 was to modify our concept, for a reality TV show. So even though we were found by news outlets, those companies were looking for money and not for moving us forward. It was all about the dollar bill before we could be on their show, or participate in their show. The next thing that I learned, or a mistake I made was I wasn't able to get any big names to support my idea or concept. I sent out numerous letters to Michael Jai White, Chuck Norris, Steven Segal and Cynthia Rothrock—there were about 20 of them. I didn't get any responses back. The one celebrity contact I did get, asked me to give up 30% of the company in ownership to him for a Chuck Norris introduction. That was just for the individual to introduce me to Chuck Norris to discuss the concept with Mr. Norris.

I met a gentleman at the Atlanta trade show who mentioned that he knew Ernest "The Cat" Miller; he said he would set up an introduction. He did that via LinkedIn. I reached out to Mr. Miller and heard nothing from him. I was convinced to try social media by a gentleman I had met at the Atlanta trade show. We let into a contract for three months. His company started posting business advertisement daily through our Facebook, Twitter and LinkedIn accounts, for three months. At the end of three months, we had 144 likes. $147 a month, we had 144 likes. At that price, I could have bought the likes through Facebook. Through LinkedIn, I got more contacts than any other medium to date. So I paid $147 a month for three months, what a waste; that was a bust. The company was SiteWise.

It would take as long as two hours for a person to fully understand my concept while talking on the phone. To me, it sounds so natural. Having played sports all of my life, it seems like this would be a next logical step for martial arts. It just seems clear cut and easy for me to understand. You have the NFL, you have major league baseball and you have the NBA, National Hockey League. All of these organizations use teams and all are professional teams. All of those teams compete through points. To add a little clarity, I would say, think of boxing in the Olympics, where they have weight classes and the different countries compete in the Olympics with the various weight categories. So you might have a lightweight from America against a lightweight from Japan, in the ring boxing. Just imagine the same with martial arts.

That's what my concept proposal is, the Pro Teams KumiteSport Martial Arts a league of martial arts teams competing against one another for a national championship. Which consists of getting the best competitors from the top 32 major tournament's black belt Kumite (fighting) divisions to form teams. The first place winners of those fighting divisions would be teamed to represent the city-state against the other 31 teams, within the Pro Teams KumiteSport Martial Arts.

I also hired an event planner that knew nothing of the industry and didn't know how to get sponsors. We had an agreement for the Columbia event. I guess my first problem was trying to host an event in Columbia. I hired an event planner. The agreement between The Pro Teams KumiteSport Martial Arts and the event planner was that she was to get sponsors for an event we were going to have in July. Per the agreement, she would be paid from sponsorship proceeds. It was clearly stated within our agreement that she would get paid from sponsor proceeds. One month before the event, we had no sponsors, and she didn't get any sponsors. For this reason, her priority should have been diligently pursuing sponsors. She said she sent 3000 emails out from her personal email account, her personal email and we waited on that. I learned later that when you send a large number of email from your own account. Most ISP's would only allow you to send 300 to 500 before they consider it spam and they close up the socket. What that means is once that number is reached the other emails don't get sent out. Approximately one month from the event, it made sense to cancel the event. Prior to that one month, we hired a company to make phone calls for us to get sponsors. I left this as a responsibility of the event planner. This was another big mistake. The event planner set everything up, the only thing, I did, was pay for the service. Six weeks before the event date I learned she had some people that needed to be called back, but the company that made the initial calls, wasn't going to make the follow-up calls. For this reason, we needed to make the calls. Since those calls were never made, we never got sponsors. That was another mistake I made. I hired somebody that wasn't knowledgeable about my industry. She apparently didn't know what it took to get sponsors. She didn't have her own sponsor list, which caused us to have to purchase the Sports Market Directory. We ended looking for sponsors using the Sports Market Directory as a reference and learned that some of the names in it had not been updated. This caused me to waste money on postage with returns and assisting the Sports Market Directory in updating their directory. That book cost around 300 dollars. Through that channel and access to their website ended up costing another $300-$500. Hiring an event planner to get sponsors actually cost me $2500. Instead of her making the necessary calls to get sponsors she convinced me to pay a company to make the phone calls to get us, sponsors. We didn't get one sponsor through the use of that company. The company hired through the event planner didn't clearly understand their role in securing sponsors. Add the $500 for the Sports Market Directory. We wasted $3000 trying to get sponsors and got nothing. A very reputable and famous brand, however, sponsored us with equipment to use at the event. So I want to thank this brand for sponsoring us for an event that never took place. I did everything I could send that equipment back to this company, but they wouldn't accept it back. They said, "We support what you are trying to do." So we now use that equipment for the Stand Up Against Violence Everywhere America (S.A.V.E. America) campaign.

I also learned that traditional martial artists actually think MMA-type events, such as the UFC, hurt martial arts. First of all, let's think about a UFC-type event. A UFC-type event, from my understanding, involves getting individuals in the ring or octagon that may not be black belts. They may learn some boxing techniques; some grappling—wrestling—jiu-jitsu, or judo techniques. Also, some type of kicking martial art: Shotokan karate, taekwondo and you have a mixed martial artist ready to fight in an MMA event. These individuals have agreed to compete within their rules, not to hurt each other with the real depths of the martial arts.

So they may learn to have an essential understanding of those techniques they then train with somebody who has trained other MMA fighters and then they get into the ring. So they may not have two to three to five to eight years' experience in that area of martial arts or have a black belt. I think a lot of the traditional martial artists feel that, because of this, this is actually hurting martial arts. I think there's a place for MMA—mixed martial arts—which I would categorize as extreme martial arts. We all know, from what we have seen over time, it depends on the individual, their dedication and how they train. Bruce Lee himself wasn't completely 100% a kung fu master but would learn from all different styles and arts to create his Jeet Kune Do. We can all agree that an individual can learn a martial art or bits and pieces of different styles, train and beat another person. That has nothing to do with the style but the person and the way he/she prepared or trained. The person's athleticism and how bad that individual wants to win, and not necessarily the style itself.

At one time, everybody thought well, you want to learn Jeet Kune Do, because of the benefits of Jeet Kune Do, or do you want to learn Dim Mak, for the death touch. But what it all boils down to is the individual, how they train and how bad they want it. I think there's always going to be a place for point martial arts. There will always be those that will never make a commitment to compete in an MMA type event or martial arts activities in which you get taken down to the ground and can possibly be pummeled into submission. It's an excellent platform for individuals that practice aikido, jiu-jitsu and judo, to showcase their skills. That's a splendid platform for them.

I learned to invest in LinkedIn it is a worthwhile investment. I've made more contacts than in any other medium, thus far, on LinkedIn. We have over 1000 contacts; those are martial arts industry specific contacts. I'm able to post an advertisement. I'm able to communicate directly with those contacts once they've accepted me as a contact. But, of course, you get more benefits with the premium package. Had I known about LinkedIn when I first franchised this concept in 2009, I probably would have sold more franchises. I probably would have found the perfect market and I wouldn't have spent so many thousands of dollars out of pocket to get where I should be.

The USA Today Newspaper, I paid $1500 for their special edition. That was a waste of money: no calls, no sales. Those are the mistakes I've made; at least those, that I felt, were mistakes. But mainly, I learned through each one of those errors. Some things I have learned, of course, as I went through that list, are things that I will not waste my time doing again. I spent a lot of time working on my website and trying to get visitors to come to it: thenationalmartialartsleague.com or thePTKMA.com.

We hired professional writers for SEO and grammar. Proper grammar and spelling allow you to communicate your message more effectively, increasing the understanding of those you are communicating with and thus increasing the chances they will take a chance on you. It also makes you look more professional. Perfection is almost impossible, but it's worth the extra effort. For a time, there I was the website designer and webmaster. In the role as a webmaster, I handled updating the site. Making all web page posts, adding the web pages, editing, adding the documentation online and everything else you can think of dealing with the site. I don't know for sure, but that may have cost me a lot of customers.

There's a wealth of information about the three franchises we offer. The master franchise allows you to own your own territory and ownership rights to your state team. Within your state, you will control the sale of other schools for your campaign to S.A.V.E. your state. Just imagine that. In the past, our focus for martial art schools had been solely within our own community. Primarily, we as teachers and instructors care about our local area. Our local communities, and the schools, the students within our schools, the teachers or instructors within our schools teaching the classes just to benefit our small space or school.

I want to challenge you to think bigger than that. Just imagine this concept: the Pro Teams KumiteSport Martial Arts as written earlier. You will be growing people from within your school to successfully secure a team position to represent their city-state, like the NFL but for the professional martial arts league. When we think of the NFL announcements that we see on TV, or when we watch a professional football game. They may announce that so-and-so went to Oklahoma University or so-and-so went to Penn State or to the University of Maryland or University of South Carolina. Those are the schools the athlete attended and played college ball. I think that's clear to everybody. That would be the same case with the Pro Teams KumiteSport Martial Arts. Joe Johnson, who may have been a student at your school—when they announce his name, for marketing, he attended your school, example... Ladies and gentlemen from, Jim Johnson's Taekwondo School out of Memphis, Tennessee, weighing in at 137 pounds and fighting in the lightweight division for the Shaolin White Snake out of Baltimore. I think over time, this can be the same marketing behemoth the NFL is, but for martial arts. A platform such as this alone will increase martial arts school enrollments, along with tournament participation. Students in your classes will aspire to end up being professional martial arts competitors, on professional martial arts teams and supporting their team like kids do for baseball, basketball and football. Remember martial arts schools are the training grounds for future talent. It's up to us to provide them a platform.

I still to this day, believe this is a tremendous opportunity for anybody willing to seize the moment. I envision opportunities for referees, judges, trainers, coaches, analysts and managers. Also, there is also an opportunity for sports medicine because we are still dealing with sports and martial arts injuries. There are opportunities for investors, team owners, school owners. I think that maybe a school owner and a team owner are different people. And the reason why I say that is because of what I've been dealing with thus far, trying to get school owners to invest in a team. Well, maybe you're a school owner and you have the capital to own a team. And if you own a team, then you would probably pick a coach and a manager to run your team while you focus on the day-to-day business or why do that? You could just hire someone and own your team and reap the benefits like other owners do.

This concept creates a tremendous opportunity for school owners in martial arts itself: reality TV at a national level, team competitions on television, like other major league sports. Mixed Martial Arts (MMA), although somewhat extreme, isn't it. It's just not a venue in my opinion that can grow martial arts to major league proportions. My reasoning is when you think of the National Football League (NFL), Major League Baseball (MLB) or the National Basketball Association (NBA), I think family entertainment. Families are able to buy tickets and go watch these events and enjoy them as a family. You can take your son to a baseball, basketball or football game. You can take your daughter to a baseball, basketball or football game, they can sit down and enjoy popcorn and drink sodas or eat hot dogs and other foods and enjoy the event. Well, that can also be the case for professional team point martial arts. We can create a platform that allows the majority of martial arts artists to compete. These would be co-ed teams, so there would be females and males and they would be from the community within which they reside, city and/ or state. I went to a movie the other day and it cost me $10.50. Spectators are comfortable with paying $10+ to watch a movie. That could be the starting price of admission to a sport martial arts team event. Of course, the closer to the ring or the closer, you are to the competition platform the more it would cost. Competitors now, they go to tournaments and pay anywhere from $35-$75 to compete. They may sit around all day long, waiting to fight, especially if they're a black belt. And then finally their time comes. Even if the entry fee were 5–6 dollars per person, it would be a start. A pro point league isn't going to grow millionaires overnight. The WNBA players started with salaries in the $40,000 per year range, semi-pro football players I heard $200 a game. I personally think starting is the first step. Salaries will build over time. Competitors are putting out the same effort and compensated very little over time the compensation will grow. My first job I got paid $1.90 an hour, I make considerably more now.

Normally, when I go to compete in a tournament and it's time for me to fight, it's around 2:30, three o'clock before I get a chance to compete. The most, I've heard of guys winning on average, is a $500 purse or $1000. We can start off with competitors on teams getting paid to $250 to $500 per event for three three-minute rounds. This is far better than what they are getting now, along with the prestige of representing their city/state in the national championship. Lebron James is heading back to Cleveland just to do that for the city he loves. I think this is an awesome opportunity and an excellent concept. I'm looking for people who want to join me in this venture.

8 A Notable Accolade

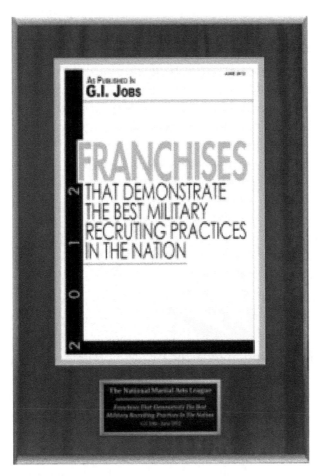

Top 10% Military Friendly Franchise Award

The Pro Teams KumiteSport Martial Arts (PTKMA) has made it to the list of the Top Military-Friendly Franchises List. This list shows that PTKMA is one of the only four franchises included in the Sports and Recreation Category. It is a list which represents the top 10% of franchises involved in recruiting and training America's Veterans as business owners. PTKMA's inclusion in this prestigious list is a testament to the marked advantage of its offering in the form of financial incentive and training for veteran franchisees. The complete list can be seen at militaryfranchising. com. It can also be seen in the June issue of G.I. Jobs and the July/August 2013 issue of Vetrepreneur Magazine.

Franchises may be owned by a corporation, partnership or by an individual and operate autonomously within the PTKMA (the League), but all teams follow the same approach in advertising and marketing. Each team develops its own identity, owns the team tryout rights for its territory to secure team members, coaches, trainers, etc. and markets accordingly. Initially, the teams need to establish themselves with media, fans, sponsors, and the ticket-buying public. Each year of operation and success enhances the overall team operation and should add to the overall appreciation of the team. PTKMA franchise teams could indeed follow the success of NFL teams, which have appreciated tenfold in the last few years. The PTKMA anticipates increasing the entry fee each year based on growth and demand. The league has recently conducted a full review of its business model, molding new strategies to better serve the long-term success of the league and its franchises within the current economic climate. The robust expansion plan underway places an emphasis on building new partnerships and competencies with other forward-looking companies, adding value to the league and its new franchises.

This venue provides a maximum opportunity for martial artists looking to showcase their skills, as well as stay in prime physical and mental condition prior to the PTKMA Team Tryouts. In addition to physical fitness and mental conditioning, the PTKMA offers excellent opportunities for coaches, referees, and front office administrative personnel seeking careers. Coaches receive experience by working with competitors and designing game strategies while judges are presented with a challenge of officiating fast-paced, action-packed professional games. People involved with management aspects gain unparalleled experience and insights into the operation of a professional sports franchise. Franchisees also become more involved with their communities by providing a professional sports team, which becomes an active vehicle for pleasure, community service, and profit.

Not only is the PTKMA a developmental forum, but it is also a revolutionary business enterprise. Established as the only point professional martial arts league to utilize franchising techniques, the PTKMA offers potential owners one of the least expensive franchises to purchase and operate in professional sports. The sensible expansion blueprint and realistic budgets allow businesspersons the opportunity to become involved at a reasonable investment level. Corporate sponsors, who seek to reap the benefits of association with professional athletics, also receive an excellent return on their investment through the achievement of reliable market value and grassroots penetration.

9 The PTKMA Player Agreement

Each winning competitor will be required to sign a one-year agreement. The agreement will be between the "Player," and the Pro Teams KumiteSport Martial Arts (PTKMA). Each competitor, although he or she will be competing for a state within the Pro Teams KumiteSport Martial Arts, he/she will be competing as a member of the Pro Teams KumiteSport Martial Arts. The Player will also sign an agreement for his/her team to compete in the PTKMA.

1. TERM. One martial arts league season(s). The season will begin the day after the event in which the competitor secures his/ her position team position, unless extended, terminated or renewed as specified elsewhere in this contract.

2. EMPLOYMENT AND SERVICES. The team aka Club will employ the competitor as a black belt or brown belt martial artist. Each player must accept such employment by signature. She/he agrees to give his/her best efforts and loyalty to the Club. To conduct him or her on and off the field with appropriate recognition of the fact that the success of this professional martial art program depends mostly on public respect for and approval of those associated with the sport. The player will report promptly for and participate fully in Club's official mandatory practices(s). All formal training and all Club meetings and practice sessions, and all preseason, regular season and postseason martial arts events scheduled for or by Club. If invited, Player will practice for and play in any all-star events sponsored by the League. The player will not participate in any martial arts activities not sponsored by nor approved by the League unless first approved by the League.

3. OTHER ACTIVITIES. Without prior written consent of the Club, Player will not participate in martial arts events or engage in activities which may involve a significant risk of personal injury. The player represents that he/she has special, exceptional and unique knowledge, skill, ability, and experience as a martial arts competitor. The loss of which cannot be estimated with any certainty and cannot be fairly or adequately compensated by damages. A player, for this reason, agrees that Club will have the right, also to any other right which Club may possess. To enjoin Player by appropriate proceedings from participating in martial arts events or engaging in martial arts-related activities other than for Club. Or from engaging in any activity other than martial arts which may involve a significant risk of personal injury.

4. PUBLICITY AND PTKMA GROUP LICENSING PROGRAM.
(a) Player grants to Club and the League, separately and together, the authority to use his name and picture for publicity and the promotion of the PTKMA, the League, or any of its member clubs. Whether be it in newspapers, magazines, motion pictures, game programs and roster manuals, broadcasts and telecasts, and all other publicity and advertising media. Provided such advertising and promotion does not constitute an endorsement by Player of a commercial product. The player will cooperate with the news media and will participate upon request in reasonable activities to promote the Club and the League. Player and the Pro Teams KumiteSport Martial Arts Players Association, from now on "PTKMAPA," will not contest the rights of the League, or its member clubs to telecast, broadcast, or otherwise transmit PTKMA events. Extended to the right of the PTKMA to produce, sell, market or distribute martial arts event film footage, except insofar as such broadcast, telecast, or transmission of footage is used in any commercially marketable event or interactive use. The League and its member clubs. Player and the PTKMAPA, reserve their respective rights to the use of such broadcasts, telecasts or transmissions of

footage in such events or interactive uses, which shall be unaffected by this subparagraph.

(b) The player at this moment assigns to the PTKMAPA and its licensing affiliates if any, the exclusive right to use and to grant to persons, firms, or corporations, (collectively "licensees"). The right to use his name, signature facsimile, voice, picture, photograph, likeness, and/or biographical information (collectively "image") in group licensing programs. Group licensing programs are defined as those licensing programs, in which a licensee utilizes a total of six (6), or more PTKMA competitor images on or in conjunction with products. Including, but not limited to, trading cards, clothing, video events, computer events, collectibles, internet sites, fantasy events, etc. That are sold at retail or used as promotional or premium items. The player retains the right to grant permission to a licensee to utilize his image. If that licensee is not concurrently using the pictures of five (5) or more other PTKMA competitors on products that sell at retail or are used as promotional or premium items. If Player's inclusion in a particular PTKMAPA program is precluded by an individual exclusive endorsement agreement, and Player provides the PTKMAPA with timely written notice of that preclusion. The PTKMAPA will exclude Player from that particular program. In consideration for this assignment of rights, the PTKMAPA will use the revenues it receives from group licensing programs to support the objectives as outlined in the Bylaws of the PTKMAPA. The PTKMAPA will use its best efforts to promote the use of PTKMA player images in group licensing programs. The PTKMAPA will provide group licensing opportunities to all PTKMA players, and to ensure that no entity utilizes the group licensing rights granted to the PTKMAPA without first obtaining a license from the PTKMAPA. This paragraph shall be construed under South Carolina law without reference to conflicts of law principles.

The assignment in this section shall expire on December 31 of the later of the third year following the execution of this contract, or the year in which this contract expires. Neither Club nor the League is a party to the terms of this paragraph, which are included within solely for the administrative convenience and benefit of Player and the PTKMAPA. The terms of this subparagraph apply unless. At the time of execution of this Contract, Player indicates by striking out this paragraph (b) and marking his initials adjacent to the stricken language his intention to not participate in the PTKMAPA Group Licensing Program. Nothing in this subparagraph shall be construed, to supersede or any way broaden, expand, detract from or otherwise alter in any way whatever, the rights of PTKMA Properties, Inc. As permitted under Article V (Union Security), Section 4 of the 1993 Collective Bargaining Agreement ("CBA").

5. COMPENSATION. For the performance of Player's services and all other promises of Player, Club will pay Player a yearly salary as follows:

$_____for the 20_____season;

$_____for the 20_____season;

$_____for the 20_____season;

$_____for the 20_____season;

$_____for the 20_____season.

Also, Club will pay Player such earned performance bonuses as may be called for in his contract. Player's reasonable board and lodging expenses during season training and in connection with playing preseason, regular season, and postseason martial arts events outside Club's home city. Player's necessary traveling expenses to and from preseason, regular season, and postseason martial arts events outside Club's hometown. Player's necessary traveling expenses to his residence if this contract is terminated by Club; and such additional compensation, benefits and reimbursement of expenses as may be called for in any collective bargaining agreement in existence during the term of this contract. (For purposes of this contract, a collective bargaining agreement will be deemed to be "in existence" during its stated time or during any period for which the parties to that agreement agree to extend it.)

6. PAYMENT. Unless this contract or any collective bargaining agreement in existence during the term of this contract expressly provides otherwise. The player will be paid 100% of his yearly salary under this contract in equal weekly or bi-weekly installments over the course of the applicable regular season period. Commencing with the first regular season event performed by Club in each season. Unless this contract expressly provides otherwise. If this contract is terminated after the beginning of the regular season, the yearly salary payable to Player will be reduced proportionately. The player will be paid the weekly or bi-weekly portions of his annual salary having become due and payable up to the time of termination.

7. DEDUCTIONS. Any advance made to Player will be repaid to Club. Any duly levied Club penalty or Commissioner imposed fine against Player will be paid, in cash on demand or using deductions from payments coming due Player under this contract. Some such deductions to be determined by Club unless this contract or any collective bargaining agreement in existence during the term of this contract expressly provides otherwise.

8. PHYSICAL CONDITION. Player will undergo a complete physical examination by the Club physician upon Club request. During his/her physical examination, Player agrees to make full and complete disclosure of any physical or mental condition is known to him which might impair his performance under this contract. Player to respond fully and in good faith when questioned by the Club physician about such condition. If Player fails to establish or maintain his excellent physical condition to the satisfaction of the Club physician. Or make the required full and complete disclosure and good faith responses to the Club physician. Then Club may terminate this contract.

9. INJURY. Unless this agreement expressly provides otherwise. If Player is injured in the performance of his services under this contract and promptly reports such damage to the Club physician or trainer. Then Player will receive such medical and hospital care during the term of this contract as the Club physician may deem necessary. Injured Player will continue to receive his yearly salary for so long, during the season of injury only and for no subsequent period covered by this contract. As Player is physically unable to perform the services required of him by this contract because of such injury. If Player's injury in the performance of his services under this contract results in his death, the unpaid balance of his yearly salary for the season of injury will be paid to his stated beneficiary. In the absence of a stated beneficiary, to his estate.

10. WORKERS' COMPENSATION. Any compensation paid to Player under this contract or under any collective bargaining agreement in existence during the term of this contract. For a period during which he is entitled to workers' compensation benefits by reason of temporary total, permanent total, temporary partial, or permanent partial disability will be deemed an advance payment of workers' compensation benefits due Player. Club will be entitled to be reimbursed the amount of such payment out of any award of employees' compensation.

11. SKILL, PERFORMANCE, AND CONDUCT. Player understands that he is competing with other players for a position on Club's roster within the applicable player limits. If at any time, in the sole judgment of Club, Player's skill or performance has been unsatisfactory as compared with that of other players competing for positions on Club's roster. If Player has engaged in personal conduct reasonably judged by Club to adversely affect or reflect on Club, then Club may terminate this contract. Also, during the period any salary cap is legally in effect. This contract may be terminated if, in Club's opinion, Player is anticipated to make less of a contribution to Club's ability to compete in events than another player or players whom Club intends to sign or attempts to sign. Or another player or players who is or are already on Club's roster, and for whom Club needs the room.

12. TERMINATION. The rights of termination outlined in this contract will be in addition to any other rights of termination allowed either party by law. Termination will be effective upon the giving of written notice. Except that Player's death, other than as a result of injury incurred in the performance of his services under this contract, will automatically terminate this contract. If this contract is terminated by Club and either Player or Club so requests, Player will promptly undergo a complete physical examination by the Club physician.

13. INJURY GRIEVANCE. Unless a collective bargaining agreement in existence at the time of termination of this contract by Club provides otherwise. The following injury grievance procedure will apply. If Player believes that at the date of termination of this contract by Club he was physically unable to perform the services required of him by because of an injury incurred in the performance of his services under this Contract. A player may, within 60 days after examination by the Club physician, submit at his own expense to examination by a doctor of his choice. If the opinion of Player's physician with respect to his physical ability to perform the services required of him by this contract is contrary to that of the Club's physician. The dispute will be submitted within a reasonable time to final and binding arbitration by an arbitrator selected by Club. If Club and Player are unable to agree on an arbitrator, one will be chosen in accordance with the procedures of the American Arbitration Association on application by either party.

14. RULES. The player will comply with and be bound by all reasonable Club rules and regulations in effect during the term of this contract which are not inconsistent with the provisions of this agreement. Or of any collective bargaining agreement in existence during the duration of this contract. Player's attention is also called to the fact that the League functions with certain rules and procedures expressive of its operation as a joint venture among its member clubs. That these standards and practices may affect Player's relationship to the League and its member clubs independently of the provisions of this contract.

15. PLAYER INTEGRITY OF THE SPORT. The Player recognizes the detriment to the League and to professional martial arts that would result from impairment of public confidence in the honest and orderly conduct of PTKMA events or the integrity and good character of PTKMA players. Player, for this reason, acknowledges his awareness that if he/she accepts a bribe or agrees to throw or fix an PTKMA event. Fails to promptly report a bribe offer or an attempt to throw or fix an PTKMA event. Bets on an PTKMA event; knowingly associates with gamblers or gambling activity; uses or provides other players with stimulants or other drugs for the purpose of attempting to enhance on-field performance, or is guilty of any other form of conduct reasonably judged by the League Commissioner to be detrimental to the League or professional martial arts. The Commissioner will have the right but only after giving Player the opportunity for a hearing. At which he may be represented by counsel of his choice, to fine Player a reasonable amount; to suspend Player for a period certain or indefinitely; and/or to terminate this contract.

16. EXTENSION. Unless this contract specifically provides otherwise, if Player becomes a member of the Armed Forces of the United States or any other country, retires from professional martial arts as an active player, or otherwise fails or refuses to perform his services under this contract. Then this contract will be tolled between the date of Player's induction into the Armed Forces or his retirement. Or his failure or refusal to perform, and the later date of his return to professional martial arts. During the period, this contract is tolled; Player will not be entitled to any compensation or benefits, on Player's return to professional martial arts. The term of this contract will be extended for a period of time equal to the number of seasons (to the nearest multiple of one) remaining at the time the contract was tolled. The right of renewal, if any, contained in this Agreement will remain in effect until the end of any such extended term.

17. ASSIGNMENT. Unless this contract specifically provides. Otherwise, Club may assign this contract and Player's services under this contract to any successor to Club's franchise or to any other Club in the League. The player will report to the assignee Club promptly upon being informed of the assignment of his contract and will faithfully perform his services under this contract. The assignee club will pay Player's necessary traveling expenses in reporting to it and will accurately perform this contract with Player.

18. FILING. This contract will be valid and binding upon Player and Club immediately upon execution. A copy of this agreement, including any attachment to it, will be filed by Club with the League Commissioner within 10 days after execution. The Commissioner will have the right to disapprove this contract on reasonable grounds. Including but not limited to an attempt by the parties to abridge or impair the rights of any other club. Uncertainty or incompleteness in the expression of the parties' respective rights and obligations or conflict between the terms of this contract and any collective bargaining agreement then in existence, approval will be automatic. Unless, within 10 days after receipt of this contract in his office, the Commissioner notifies the parties either of disapproval or of extension of this 10-day period for purposes of investigation or clarification pending his decision. On the receipt of notice of disapproval and termination, both parties will be relieved of their respective rights and obligations under this contract.

19. DISPUTES. During the term of any collective bargaining agreement, any dispute between Player and Club, involving the interpretation or application of any provision of this contract, will be submitted to final and binding arbitration in accordance with the procedure called for in any collective bargaining agreement in existence at the time the event giving rise to any such dispute occurs.

20. NOTICE. Any notice, request, approval or consent of this contract will be sufficiently given in writing and delivered in person or mailed, (certified or first class), by one party to the other at the address set forth in this contract or to such other address as the recipient may subsequently have furnished in writing to the sender.

21. OTHER AGREEMENTS. This contract, including any attachment to it, sets forth the entire agreement between Player and Club and cannot be modified or supplemented orally. Player and Club represent that no other agreement, oral or written. Except as attached to or expressly incorporated in this contract, exists are conflicting provisions in any collective bargaining agreement in existence during the term of this contract, in which case the provisions of the collective bargaining agreement will take precedence over conflicting provisions of this contract relating to the rights or obligations of either party.

22. LAW. This Agreement is made under and shall be governed by the laws of the State of_____.

23. WAIVER AND RELEASE. Player waives and releases any claims that he may have arising out of, related to, or asserted in the lawsuit entitled White v. Pro Teams KumiteSport Martial Arts, including, but not limited to, any such claim regarding past PTKMA Rules. The first refusal/compensation system, the PTKMA COMPETITOR AGREEMENT, preseason compensation, or any other term or condition of employment, except any claims, asserted in Brown v. Pro Martial Arts, Inc. This waiver and release also extend to any conduct engaged in pursuant to the Stipulation and Settlement Agreement. This waiver and release shall not limit any rights Player may have to competing by the Club, under this Contract during its review by the court in____. This waiver and release are subject to Article XIV (PTKMA COMPETITOR AGREEMENT), Section 3(c) of the NCA.

24. OTHER PROVISIONS. (a) Each of the undersigned at this moment confirms, that (I) this contract, renegotiation, extension or amendment sets forth all components of the player's remuneration for playing professional martial arts. Whether such compensation is being furnished directly by the Club or by a related or affiliated entity. There are not undisclosed agreements of any kind. Whether express or implied, oral or written. There are no promises, undertakings, representations, commitments, inducements, assurances of intent, or understandings of any kind that have not been disclosed to the PTKMA involving consideration of any kind to be paid, furnished or made available to Player or any entity or person owned or controlled by, affiliated with, or related to Player, either during the term of this contract or thereafter. (b) Each of the undersigned further confirms that except insofar as any of the undersigned may describe in an addendum to this contract. To the best of their knowledge, no conduct in violation of the Anti-Collusion rules of the Settlement Agreement took place with respect to this contract. Each of the undersigned further confirms that nothing in this contract is written or intended to defeat or circumvent any provisions of the Settlement Agreement. Including but not limited to Salary Cap rules; however, any conduct permitted by the Settlement Agreement shall not be considered a violation of this confirmation. (c) The Club further confirms that any information regarding the negotiation of this contract that it provided to the Neutral Verifier was, at the time the information was provided, genuine and correct in all material respects. There are standard terms & conditions that must be followed.

10 Frequently Asked Questions

What Up Front Investment is Required?

Depending on your franchise choice and territory your franchise fee could range anywhere from $25,000 to $75,000. This is a one-time payment and is determined by the size of the area purchased. Also, there are the costs associated with setting up your Stand-Up Against Violence (S.A.V.E.) America or plug in your city Training Facility. There is also the cost of travel to Columbia, SC for a 5-day training program.

Royalty Fee

The royalty fee is a minimum Fee of $1000 per month. Fees are paid by Stand-Up Against Violence Everyone (S.A.V.E.) America or plug in your city franchisees. A fee of 6% of gross revenues shall be paid from the Pro Teams KumiteSport Martial Arts Franchise revenues. These costs were determined by the franchise development company we used to franchise our business model. We are no longer under contract with them and have more flexibility and room for negotiation in all future franchise sales.

Marketing Fund Contributions

Paid by franchisees—A royalty of 3% of gross revenues shall be paid to the Franchiser from the Pro Teams KumiteSport Martial Arts Franchise revenues. A total of 9% of all gross income goes to the main company,

6% goes to growing the corporate business, with 3% for marketing. A national campaign will be needed to sustain the professional point martial arts league.

What Return on Investment (ROI) can I Expect?

The actual up-front investment to open A Pro Teams KumiteSport Martial Arts Team Franchise or Stand-Up Against Violence (S.A.V.E.) your city franchise is relatively small in comparison to other professional franchises. Yes, but the ROI is also considerably lower. NFL franchise or team owners can expect MILLIONS to come in from advertisers and other companies, which allow them to pay their players. That's also why it COSTS millions to buy these teams. A professional point league can also gain advertisers, sponsors and investors just as do other sports given the same time for growth, resources and funding for marketing. PTKMA Franchise S.A.V.E. your city franchises are entirely dependent on the expectation and needs of the Franchisee. It is impossible to give you an exact ROI. However, the immediate source of cash flow is created as new students or members are pre-enrolled prior to your grand opening. This allows a positive cash flow to be established quickly.

How Quickly can I Expect a Return on My Investment to Begin?

As soon as you sign your lease and start pre-selling in your exclusive territory, you can start to recover your initial investment by enrolling new students/members.

How Many Employees do I Need?

You can start with as little as two people including yourself, as owner/manager, salesperson, and an instructor. However, Franchisees, who have the funds to hire additional people whose talents complement their own can grow faster, also, Area Developer Franchisees many need additional personnel.

What Type of Facility do I Need?

You will need approximately 3500–4000 Sq. Ft. for the school/teen scene and a small office. The facility must be sprinkled; you'll need signage, phone, a PC running a Windows operating system, and high-speed Internet access.

What Type of Technology (Phone, Fax, Computer and the Internet) do I Need?

You will need a Personal Computer. Your internet connection should be one of the various high-speed options: DSL, cable or satellite.

How Long has the Pro Teams KumiteSport Martial Arts been in Business?

The franchise company was started in November of 2009 to launch the Pro Teams KumiteSport Martial Arts.

How much Support will I Receive after the Initial Training and Specifically, How does The Pro Teams KumiteSport Martial Arts Franchise Support My Business?

The National Martial Arts Franchise provides you with a web-based infrastructure for the billing, collection and servicing of student-member accounts. The technology provides reports for your school and teams activities as well as administrative functions. Also, a Pro Teams KumiteSport Martial Arts Franchise offers various Franchisee service departments to handle Franchisee questions and concerns. As a Franchisee, you will have a team of support staff to assist you in operating your Franchise.

What are the Key Drivers of the Business— the Essential Skills Needed?

As much fun and as exciting at the Pro Teams KumiteSport Martial Arts Franchise opportunity is, it is certainly not for everyone. You will need to be involved on a full-time basis, and you will be rewarded for your efforts and time commitment. The most successful franchises and martial arts schools have been operated by energetic team leaders with some business and management experience. Your Franchise Agreement requires you to hire certified black belt instructors and approved managers. Following the Pro Teams KumiteSport Martial Arts Franchise system is critical to your success as a franchisee.

What Competition should I Expect?

Simmons Market Research shares that martial arts participation has increased 5% within the past year; however that does not translate to tournament competition for many reasons. One of which is there isn't a level of competition beyond the amateur sport. There are over 50,000 established conventional karate schools, MMA centers, gyms and fitness centers throughout America. The Pro Teams KumiteSport Martial Arts Franchise offers something no other franchise offers. The PTKMA Franchise offers a solutions-based martial arts campaign in its quest to S.A.V.E. America along with a team league system combined with providing genuine territorial rights and a support system. There is very little market penetration for franchised karate school-type businesses, but the interest and the potential audience is growing faster than most other sporting activity franchises.

Will I Receive a Protected Territory?

Yes, you will receive an exclusive, protected territory (Protected from other PTKMA franchises, not competitors from other franchises or independent facilities.). You will be assigned a protected area based upon a 100,000 population density. Generally, we will not place another franchise within 20 miles of the location of your Pro Teams KumiteSport Martial Arts Franchise except your supported franchise domain.

How do I Generate Income?

As a franchisee, you should be successful in generating income through the following programs:

- Teen Scene monthly club memberships
- Bringing in new student members

- Self-defense basic membership
- Self-defense advanced membership
- Don't Bully Me summer camps
- Selling martial arts equipment
- Special events (FightNite)
- Build Your Dream Body memberships
- Providing upgraded classes and personal training for student-members

If This is such a Great Opportunity, why haven't I Heard of You Before?

The Pro Teams KumiteSport Martial Arts Franchise philosophy has just been defined, documented and registered November 2009, in preparation for the franchise program to be launched nationwide.

What will Cause My Pro Teams KumiteSport Martial Arts Franchise Business to Grow Quickly?

Aggressive advertising, regular community outreach activities, sales, and marketing will build an active, stable business with good quality student members who renew their memberships. Also, following proven systems provided by the Pro Teams KumiteSport Martial Arts Franchise and only hiring Pro Teams KumiteSport Martial Arts Franchise approved managers and class instructors will expedite your success. We have been successful in putting together an authorized business plan that will allow all owners the opportunity to get funded by the Small Business Administration (SBA). Also, our Franchise Disclosure Documents have also been approved so that any individual interested in purchasing a franchise team w/school can be funded as well. The biggest piece of the puzzle is to get funded we've been able to get approvals for all interested parties relieving them of the hassle and frustration. I think that's worth talking about.

What Dynamics is Essential to Consider in Determining if I'm in a Good Market?

Based on our researched data which was required by the Small Business Administration (SBA), to get the approval of our business plan. Owners will need to locate their franchise, within a populated area base of 100,000 people. Within a 5–7 miles radius of the company, where the average annual household income is of at least $35,000 and a mix of age groups.

What's My Next Step?

- Complete the Franchise Application and return it to:
  The Pro Teams KumiteSport Martial Arts Franchise,
  LLC 208 Majestic Drive,
  Columbia, SC 29223

- Or email:
  dexterkennedy@hotmail.com

Upon Receipt of My Application, What Happens Next?

We will contact you to discuss your request and when all are in agreement, we will send you a Franchise Disclosure Document (FDD) to continue the franchising process. If there continues to be mutual interest, you will be scheduled a phone interview and possibly an invitation to our corporate office.

11 Franchise Interest

I n this section, you'll find email correspondence from numerous individuals that have shared their comments, enthusiasm and interest in a professional point martial arts league.

Busy but well my friend. How have you been? I was writing in hopes that Ix could become a member and/or representative of your organization. I will send you my resume/bio soon. Until then, please feel free to visit my website below. Believe and Achieve,

Grandmaster B. Y. http://www.--------.com

Hi Dexter,

It was great talking to you last week and learning more about the PTKMA project. I'm still interested. I wanted to give you a copy of my resume so you can familiarize yourself with my business background. I have not updated it since changing companies about 8 months ago, so it's a little outdated. As we discussed on the phone, I've been a hobby student in various martial arts gyms for the last 20 years of my life, as well. I would love to learn a little more about your background as we move forward. Lastly, a couple of items I was thinking about after our phone conversation. Do you have an information packet or booklet that lay out some of the concepts, etc. for potential owners? Is there a business plan or estimated P&L/financial sheet to look at? Thanks!

- J. W.

Hello,

I am interested in Maryland, Virginia, Pennsylvania, Tennessee, North Carolina, South Carolina, California, and Nevada. Thank you.

- W. J. D.

PS-I am also in the US Army Reserves and have an MOS of Military Police (31B) and Human Resource Specialist (42A) would that be a problem? Thank you again.

My name is T. B.

I am the head instructor of B. P., M.A. Please send me information on the League franchise.

I do not have my own school but would like to recommend my Instructor: Hanshi James E. White, Universal Karate Studios, Karate-Do, Lancaster, SC. He would be an excellent choice for this opportunity as he has over 40 years of experience in martial arts. This would be of great interest to him.

R. W., Student,
U. Karate Studios

Hello!

This sounds like a fun project! Not sure if it would be something we would mobilize on, but you never know.

Can you tell me how do you envision it working from a business standpoint? Also, where are you located? Why isn't Hawaii included? I am interested in Oregon, my second home.

Best Regards,

M. L.

Dexter Kennedy wrote:

Hey M., sorry for the late response. 1: yes there is a buy-in fee, but it depends on what level your existing school is at. These are actual real franchise opportunities listed on the franchise registry. I went through the extra effort to make this a genuine investment opportunity. Also, there are franchise fees to help grow the league so that it can grow to the level of the other major league franchises. Prices can range from $25,000–$277,000; of course, the latter is for an entirely new setup. 2: the team will be determined by the first place Black Belt winners within your state at an annual tournament to determine the best of the best to represent your state. The registration fees will provide you revenue to build your team and organization. 3: There will be only one league. For over 70 years in America sport, martial arts have been practiced. There are over 500 amateur circuits, over 40,000 martial arts schools in America. Don't you think it's time for a professional circuit? Individuals can continue to compete in the amateur circuits until they secure a professional team position. I hope these answers provide you what you need as far as understanding the growth potential of a professional point martial arts league (PPMAL). Please share with me any other questions you may have.

Thanks in advance,

D. K.

Dexter,

Hi Sir, I have also had the desire to expand the professionalism of martial arts competition as well and have formed an organization and had been working towards getting into the marketplace. I have other ideas as well to capture another market which I would discuss with you in person. I want to hear more about what you are proposing. I am interested in being an active force in helping create it. I believe your invitation was found because of the law of attraction and I know that together a partnership would work to bring about something that would be spectacular. I can be reached at (xxx) xxx-xxxx and will have time to talk this afternoon around 3pm. I am also available to discuss via email.

Sincerely,
F. K.
P. Martial Arts Fitness
Fighting ~ Self-Defense
www.--------.com

The Pro Teams KumiteSport Martial Arts is seeking a Team owner for the North Carolina Pro Sports Team Link J. A. T., Sr. responded: Please forward information regarding franchises with The Pro Teams KumiteSport Martial Arts. Thank you. My respect for you and The Martial Arts...

On 2013-12-4, L. H. wrote:

Want to call you. Please send me a phone number that I can return a Call to you. Thank You

On 2013-11-2, 14:52, B. Y. wrote:

I would be interested in becoming a martial arts tournament promoter for the state of Ohio.

―――――――――

Mr. B.,

Thank you for providing me with potential team owners for the New York Team. I will keep you posted as our league progresses. If you should have any questions or need additional information as you speak of this opportunity, please feel free to contact me.

Yours truly,
Dexter Kennedy, President,
The Pro Teams KumiteSport Martial Arts, LLC

―――――――――

On 2013-7-29, 14:49, W. M. wrote:

Is your franchise registered with the SBA? If not, you should consider this. The SBA is the best way to finance franchises.

Sincerely,
W. M.
Vice President Commercial &
Government Guaranteed Lending
---- Bank
Philadelphia, PA 19129

―――――――――

Good day, Mr. Kennedy,

My name is V. B.; I am a 3rd Dan Black belt instructor from South Africa. I came across your brochure and am very interested in your concept as I have been planning my own League in South Africa called "League."

Please advise if there is any way we can bring your concept to South Africa as there is a huge market on this side. There are no professional karate Leagues, and yet there are thousands of karateka.

Thanking you in karate
Sensei V. B.
(xxx) xxx-xxxx

———●————————————————●———

Hello, Mr. Kennedy,

Thanks for your rapid response, I am a combat veteran who got injured in battle and suffers from PTSD, and I have a family of 5. Finding employment after the Army has been very difficult so I came across this opportunity in a bunch of Vet friendly franchises. Everything sounds interesting but to not waste your time or my time. What do you fully offer for Vets?

Thanks,
L. M.
(xxx) xxx-xxxx
El Paso, TX

———●————————————————●———

On 2013-7-10, K. wrote:

Great I love the concept how can I be a part of this? I would like to set a meeting up with who is in charge of your circuit…I have a concept I developed 5 years ago that might benefit us by working together. Thank you for your correspondence.

S. C., CEO
XXX Events LLC
xxxxxx@xxxxx.com

Mr. Kennedy,

It was a pleasure conversing with you the other day, after typing in your email address; I think you could have come up with a longer one, (LOL). Well, let me first provide a little insight on who I am. My arts foundation is in boxing, my Dad fought and taught in the Army.

So my first memories are of sporting boxing gloves. Growing up in the sixties had its pros' and cons'; I seemed to gravitate towards the cons'. In my heart, I have always known that I was destined to a greater purpose. So in my early teens I found the Martial Arts as more significant positive, than all the negatives I was currently living in my life. I saw the arts as a vehicle for a better life. Health through physical exertion and mental as well as social preparation towards progression in a functional and meaningful life. Mentally I improved my self-esteem, confidence, discipline and the willingness to learn and provide my teaching to others. Socially, the tenants of the martial arts were showing me how one should treat others and develop integrity in the things I did personally and publically. After years of experience in the arts, I have learned and seen that most, "real artists" are splendid people. Down to earth, evenly keeled and prepared to help their fellow man. I personally feel that the arts have provided me the opportunity to see the world, make money and help untold numbers of people. What more could one ask for? My feelings are that seeing our arts becoming more commonplace would inevitably provide more peace and harmony globally. If everyone knew how to act and treat others, how could there possibly be any conflict? The problem with most professional sports is that money and notoriety are first and foremost; because the arts include factors that most sports leave out. Honor, Respect, Courtesy, Compassion and real role model leading. If most people learned the proper value of humanity that protrudes in the arts, then most negativity would dissipate. Training relieves tension, good instruction provides leadership that is easily imitated and passed on. Imagine leagues across the country leading by example, passing on positive traits as well as a profession that one could lead well into their elder years. A controlled, exciting, contact sport where devastating injury is not common. The spectator wins through entertainment and the competitors win through longevity not only in sport but as a way of life. What more could we all ask for? Entertainment, Safety, Finance, A Positive Way of Life and Seeds to Sow to the Masses. How many times have you heard of a true Martial Artist being involved in something negative? So in my opinion a country of Professional Martial Artists, could only help our World become the Better Place in Which to Live. I look forward to the Pro Teams KumiteSport Martial Arts.

D. H.
Founder, xxxxxxxxxxx.com

———————•———————

DK,

I am interested in competing. I weigh about 170. I am 43 years young and in excellent shape for my age. I started taking karate at 10 years old and have practiced many styles including go ju shorin, boxing, kickboxing, Muay Thai, and taekwondo. I have placed and won numerous tournaments. I won 2 gold and 1 silver medal at the NC State Games. I was a sparring partner for Lemont Davis, 2 times World Champion Kickboxer (KICK Association) and a World Combat League fighter (Chuck Norris's League). I always love the melee and do not understand the trend in schools these days who find sparring optional. I would love to get connected with some people who like to fight and compete. Feel free to pass my name along to someone who may be looking for a team member. I attached a few pics from the final dress rehearsal of a production called Xxx Xxxxx. Thanks!

D. V.

Dear Mr. C.,

It appears you and I have been working on the same project from two entirely different avenues. I would appreciate a brief conference with you at your leisure, of course. Oh, I'm sorry you don't know who I am exactly…that's been my challenge. Nobody knows who I am, and that's the reason I can't get my business off the ground. When you have time Google, "Get Paid to Compete," "Dexter Kennedy" or "professionalizing sport martial arts." I've been working on this project since 2002, which is well before Chuck Norris' started the World Combat League. I hope to hear from you, the sooner, the better but I'm sure that you are a busy man, and if you don't have the time I'll understand. Thanks in advance,

Dexter V. Kennedy, President,
The Pro Teams KumiteSport Martial Arts, LLC
http://www.thePTKMA.com
Cell Phone: (xxx) xxx-xxxx

Friends in Martial Arts, Hello Mr. Kennedy,

Thank you for your interest in the sport of martial arts. Having been in the martial arts business for over 40 years, I can tell you that MMA is one of the worse things that have happened to our image as a martial artist. Schools that have added MMA classes to their product line have found that the MMA clientele have little or no respect for students of the more traditional arts, and sometimes make rude comments or belittle their traditional ways. Many of them have discontinued those classes. I work with over 20 schools on the east coast that were tournament schools that have turned away from them due to the amount of time and money that tournaments take up and take away from their businesses. We have learned that students are willing to attend in-house school tournaments more frequently and pay the same fees, without the travel. The instructor makes an extra $1,000 every couple of months. The students get the trophies and medals, the parents S.A.V.E money, and the teachers and instructors can focus on things besides skills for winning an open tournament. As in all mainstream sports, they are promoted because of the profits that they earn from little league up. Why else would a high school support a sport like football where there has to be an ambulance setting ready for the game!? Do you know how many concussions children get every year from football and baseball? The real value of our program is not who can beat who, but what it does in helping others experience the other values that are taught such as courtesy, respect, confidence and becoming an intelligent leader. Good luck with the PTKMA and thanks for your leadership in the martial arts community.

Sincerely,
L. A.

Master Kennedy,

You raise a good point, sir. I am not interested at this time because my school went under, but I am still training and still provide seminars. I wish you well with your Sport Karate tournaments and would love to see karate keep rising. Karate is well promoted and style that has a lot of competitors in some states... I always say it's not the style it is the student... For myself, I can't afford to hit a circuit of a form and compete for the season anymore. So the 1–2,or sometimes 3 a year I can do. I look for the division that fits my style Continuous or point sparring, ground submissions, self-defense, weapons kata, open hand kata. A lot of styles have 500 divisions but mostly katas and point sparring... I like this style more than MMA. A lot of them are street thugs looking for fights. They miss out on the main principles of respect, discipline and honoring the history of martial arts. The majority of the talented fighters on TV from the UFC or whatever come from karate or a style of martial arts...

Respect and Honor
R. Y.

———————•———————

On 2012-5-27, O. P. wrote:

Ok, what can I do to help...what do you need from me, I don't compete anymore. I just teach, judge and referee at competitions. I fell out of the industry because I needed to find ways to make money to feed my family. However, if I can help, feel free to email me or text or call, I am an instructor (AL'I) 5th Dan.

———————•———————

Dexter:

I am still waiting to hear back from you in regards to joining up.

M.

———————•———————

Dexter,

If you would, send me your phone number. I want to run a couple of ideas by you that may make it easier to get the teams complete. Thanks! D. V.

Great questions Dexter, Let me explain a bit more. First, with Pro Martial Arts. Yes, they show up on the registry because they have what's called FRUNS #, which is a unique identifier like a Dun and Bradstreet number. The FRUNS# is assigned by our information management team, and the only reason, you don't have one right now, is because we've never had an FDD of yours. As for the FRAN data website listings of those brands, people can order their FDD's from our website; those have nothing to do with being an approved brand on the registry. There's a bit of confusion regarding the registry I think. Don't think of it as a "yes/ no" for getting approved. It's not a gamble or anything like that. What will happen is you'll receive comments from the SBA on any control/eligibility issues they find. Then you will work in conjunction with them to create a fix addendum to these matters, whatever they may be. This addendum will be pulled from the registry by lenders and used in the SBA loan process. So, basically what I'm saying is they will never just say, "No, not approved," and you eat the $2,500. We work to ensure that your brand gets approved and meets their eligibility guidelines. The only instance, I can remember where a brand submitted an agreement for review and was not accepted, was T. K. They should have never tried however because their policy of only hiring female waitresses is an issue for discriminatory purposes. So basically they reviewed the document, sent comments mentioning this fact, and Tilted Kilt decided they weren't obviously going to change this policy if you've ever been there you'd understand why. There is a pre-screening questionnaire that will give you an idea of the areas they'll be looking for regarding control issues. Good idea going to the SBA office to discuss. Does anything here not make sense?

—T.

T.,

Thanks for the information. I'm currently reviewing the data you sent and perusing the websites. A few things I've noticed.—On the franchise registry although pro martial arts is not an approved brand on the registry they have a funs# that allows them to be listed. I'm sure that works in their favor.— On the Fran data website I see the following competitors that I wasn't aware of are listed as having their franchise disclosure documents available for review: xxx, xxx, xxx, etc. I'd like to know how to get added to both of these lists. In addition, I would also like to better understand why I would not be considered for approval as a brand on the registry? Ok, so after I've paid the $2500 for the review of my franchise documents, and do not meet the requirements for approval, will the $2500 be refunded or are these funds lost? What in my FDD documents could prevent me from being approved? Is there a pre-screening of these documents so I'll get an idea of what if any changes are needed prior to the application review and before paying the $2500? I'm interested in moving forward but don't want to lose my investment if there's no chance that my franchise could be an approved brand on the registry. Lastly, I'm going to visit my local SBA and ask them a few questions about the Franchise Registry and get a better understanding of how Fran data is used.

Thanks in advance, DK

•———————————•

Dexter,

See the attached memo and lender testimonial. The notice gives the broad strokes on what the Franchise Registry does for your brand as you anticipate growing your business. In a nutshell, being an approved brand on the Franchise Registry facilitates the SBA lending process for your franchisees. They are ultimately pre-approved for SBA financing as your agreement will have been reviewed and deemed to be in full compliance with SBA eligibility standards after you work with the SBA to fix any issues they may find. Being an approved brand on the registry basically makes you a much more attractive investment for potential franchisees. It will show them, the investor that you have taken the appropriate measures to ensure to them that they will be treated as a small business owner. It makes you more competitive amongst your peers; we've already noted that your prime competitor is not an APPROVED brand on the registry, so this would again make you more attractive to potential franchisees. Does all this make sense? I hope I haven't been too wordy; I do that sometimes. Let's discuss tomorrow, is there anytime that works for you, in particular?

T. K.

Client Solutions Specialist

Re: Merger Network Listing xxx-xxxxxx
MMA Sports Team Franchise for Sale Connecticut

Hello—interested to take a look; ML This message was delivered to dkennedy@thenationalmartialartsleague. com as well as your MergerNetwork.com inbox. Hello, I am interested in PTKMA franchising. How the league is set up, schedule, what locations are already taken, start date, etc.? Do franchisees have to use the names of teams provided? Your response would be appreciated. Thank you,

Sincerely, B.

B.,

Thank you for your inquiry. The league itself initially is to comprise of 32 teams, the first 32 locations to commit will be "the League." In answer to your question, The League has no schedule as of this date. The PTKMA has spent the past few years setting up retirement opportunities and benefits. Selecting martial arts school and franchise software. Ensuring funding is available for those interested. Getting listed on the franchise registry (allowing potential franchisees the opportunity to get a 75% loan guarantee through the Small Business Administration) to benefit future franchisees.

There haven't been any franchises sold as of this date, but there has been much interest. The team concept along with the two event strategies are an opportunity to create excitement in the point martial arts arena. To allow amateur tournament competitors the chance to graduate to the professional ranks. An opportunity missed through MMA. I hope this response helps in your decision and peaks your interest more,

Thank you,
The PTKMA

Glossary

Black belt - The rank of an expert in a martial art such as judo or karate. A person who has attained this level.

Blood clock - The clocked time for an injured competitor to stop bleeding.

Brown belt - A brown belt marking a high level of proficiency in judo, karate, or other martial arts, below that of a black belt.

Diaspora - A group of people who live outside the area in which they had lived for a long time or in which their ancestors lived.

Etymology - An explanation of where a word came from the history of a word.

Jiu-jitsu, jujutsu or jujitsu - An art of weaponless self-defense developed in Japan that uses throws, holds, and blows and derives added power from the attacker's own weight and strength.

Lance - A long weapon for thrusting, having a wooden shaft and a pointed steel head, formerly used by a horseman in charging.

Medu-neter - Kemetic (ancient Egyptian) and it means, "Words of God."

Muay Thai **or Thai Boxing** - is the cultural martial art of Thailand. The origin of Muay Thai dates back several hundred years and was, essentially, developed as a form of close-combat that used the entire body as a weapon.

Sensei - A Japanese word that is literally translated as "a person born before another." In general usage, it is used, with proper form. After

153

an individual's name and means "teacher," and the word is used as a title to refer to or address teachers, professors, professionals such as lawyers, CPA and doctors, politicians, clergymen, and other figures of authority. The word is also used to show respect to someone who has achieved a certain level of mastery in an art form or some other skill, i.e. accomplished puppeteers, novelists, musicians, and artists, for example, are addressed in this way.

Shin guard - A protective covering, usually of leather or plastic. Often padded, for the shins and sometimes the knees, worn chiefly by catchers in baseball and goalkeepers in ice hockey.

Taekwondo - A Korean martial art that emphasizes powerful kicks.

White belt - A white cloth waistband is worn by a beginner in a martial art.

About the Author

Dexter V. Kennedy is the founder and president of the Pro Teams KumiteSport Martial Arts (PTKMA), LLC. He is also a retired Warrant Officer from the United States Army.

As a young boy, Dexter too, like most young boys, dreamed of playing in the NFL. As a young boy living in Baltimore, the neighborhood kids would gather around and play football in the yard on the side of his parents' home. Born a dependent he would have to learn to make friends and who to trust even faster. Dexter truly loved the sport of football and would pattern his play after the football comic the Baltimore Freight train when he played with the Mary Dobkin Colts. A sports program tailored for the inner city youth of Baltimore. He would later play baseball and basketball. Dexter learned later in life from his father that his real talent was in baseball.

As a dependent Dexter would live in Bamberg, Germany; Nuremberg and Munich Germany; Fort Sill, Oklahoma; Aberdeen, Maryland and Milwaukee, Wisconsin before returning to his parents' home in South Carolina. He would attend Eau Claire High School become class president and a star fullback to later tear the cartilage in his knee in the Lower Richland game never to play organized football again. The injury would take him down a new path which was music. Dexter started the first neighborhood band, which later transformed into a performing group under Marvin Mann of Manpower Productions. As time passed performing with the band would lose its newness.

At the young age of sixteen and the release of the movie *Fists of Fury* starring Bruce Lee, Dexter found martial arts. Dexter first started taking lessons in taekwondo and later that same year changed to Isshinryu karate. Isshinryu is an Okinawan art form that was being taught by Mike Genova. Although he learned the Okinawan art his school was focused primarily in American Freestyle Karate, Dexter found his true love in forms competition and became the star of forms competition for Genova Karate Studio. In 1977, he enlisted in the United States Army in hopes of competing in the Olympics and being trained by Mike Echanis. After two years on Kelly Hill, Fort Benning, Georgia he was assigned to the 8th Infantry Division location Baumholder, Germany also known as "the Rock." During Dexter's tour in Baumholder, Germany, he would himself represent his unit in a community boxing smoker. His win would open future opportunities for him to box on the Posts boxing team. After his stint in Europe Dexter changed career fields from Infantry to computers, receiving his initial training at Fort Gordon in Augusta, Georgia. After graduation, his first duty assignment was with the 364th Division Supply Unit (DSU) located at the Knox Street Warehouse, Fort Bragg, North Carolina. He served in Desert Storm with the 24th Infantry Division in

1990 and later served as a mainframe systems instructor at Fort Gordon, retiring from the U.S. Army in 1994.

In his search for something to do to stay fit, Dexter found his way back to the martial arts. This time through Kumite and not forms, his first tournament being the Battle of Atlanta, he was disqualified during his first fight for malicious contact. Dexter later found a sparring partner in Jimmy Sherman and they started seeking tournaments. They chose to travel the National Blackbelt League (NBL) circuit. After seven years of being rated 1 and 2 he realized he wanted more and felt there might be others. This is approximately when the Holy Spirit spoke to him and shared the vision for the Pro Teams KumiteSport Martial Arts. As you can see, his concept has been very well thought out with a clear career path for martial arts and martial artists. Thank you and enjoy!

Connect with Dexter Kennedy

Social Media

I really appreciate you reading my book!
Here are my social media coordinates:

Friend me at
www.facebook.com/nationalmartialartsleague

Follow me on Twitter:
http://twitter.com/theNMAL

Connect on LinkedIn:
www.linkedin.com/in/theNMAL

Business Contact Information

Mailing address:
Dexter V. Kennedy, President
The Pro Teams KumiteSport Martial Arts, LLC
208 Majestic Drive
Columbia, SC 29223

Email address:
dexterkennedy@hotmail.com

Cell phone: **(803) 665-8453**

Notes

Notes

Notes

Notes

_____
_____
_____
_____
_____
_____
_____
_____
_____
_____
_____
_____
_____
_____
_____
_____
_____
_____
_____
_____
_____
_____

Notes

Notes

_____

_____

_____

_____

_____

_____

_____

_____

_____

_____

_____

_____

_____

_____

_____

_____

_____

_____

_____

_____